The Smart Future

AI Foundations

The Smart Future

AI Foundations

Sergio Ramírez Gallardo

Index

## Chapter 1

Introduction to Advanced Artificial Intelligence

Artificial Intelligence (AI) has revolutionized the way we interact with technology and the world around us. From product recommendations on e-commerce platforms to innovations in autonomous driving, AI has proven to have a profound and transformative impact on various industries. However, as we move towards a future where AI becomes increasingly sophisticated, it is essential to understand what advanced artificial intelligence really entails, its objectives, and potential.

Contextualization of Advanced AI

Advanced AI represents a significant step beyond traditional AI methods. While basic AI can handle specific and well-defined tasks, advanced AI is capable of addressing more complex problems, adapting, and learning from new situations and data over time. This advancement is made possible by technological innovations and the development of more sophisticated algorithms that enable deep learning and process optimization.

A good example of this evolution can be observed in recommendation systems. Previously, these applications used simple algorithms based on collaborative filtering. However, with advancements in AI and deep learning, they can now evaluate consumption patterns, analyze sentiments, and predict future purchases in a much more effective and accurate manner, while simultaneously providing personalized recommendations for each user.

Key Characteristics of Advanced AI

One of the most notable features of advanced AI is its ability to learn from large amounts of unstructured data. This type of data includes text, images, sound, and a variety of forms of information that do not easily fit into conventional data structures. The ability of advanced AI to process, understand, and extract patterns from this information allows it to surpass the limitations of simpler forms of AI.

Additionally, the implementation of artificial intelligence models using deep neural networks has enabled notable advances in natural language processing and computer vision. For example, neural network-based systems have achieved levels of accuracy in image classification tasks that exceed human capabilities.

Introduction to Artificial General Intelligence (AGI)

A comprehensive concept in the realm of advanced AI is Artificial General Intelligence (AGI). Unlike specialized AI, which is trained to perform specific, defined tasks, AGI aims to build systems capable of learning and applying knowledge across a wide variety of tasks, functioning similarly to a human being. This objective, while ambitious, could radically transform human-machine interaction and offer AI systems greater autonomy and flexibility.

Consider how a human applies their learning across diverse areas; an engineer who understands mathematical principles can over time learn about physics or economics using their foundational knowledge. AGI seeks to replicate this versatility, a challenge that still faces enormous technical and ethical difficulties.

Challenges in Developing Advanced AI

Reaching this level of sophistication in AI is fraught with considerable obstacles. One of the main issues is the optimization of algorithms. As AI models become increasingly complex, the need for greater computational power and effective optimization techniques becomes a critical requirement to ensure efficient learning and accurate predictions. For example, adjusting appropriate hyperparameters in complex models, such as deep neural networks, can be a monumental task and requires advanced search and tuning methodologies.

Another significant challenge is obtaining large volumes of data for training models. The quality and quantity of data directly impact the effectiveness of AI models. Currently, the collection and curation of data can not only be a costly process but also labor-intensive. Furthermore, there is an urgent need to address ethical considerations related to the management of this information.

For example, when developing an AI model aimed at detecting fraud in financial transactions, it is crucial to ensure that the information used to train that model does not contain biases, as this could lead to unfair or inaccurate decisions in practice.

Conclusion

Advanced artificial intelligence elevates the need for sophisticated and efficient algorithms to a new level. Throughout this book, we will explore various techniques and approaches that will enable us to tackle these challenges and move towards AI models that are not only effective but also capable of learning, adapting, and evolving continuously in response to new data and situations. Understanding these fundamental concepts is key to maximizing the potential of AI in a rapidly transforming world.

## Chapter 2

Fundamentals of Reinforcement Learning

Reinforcement learning is a fascinating area within the field of artificial intelligence that is inspired by how humans and animals learn through experience. This approach is based on the idea that an agent can learn to make decisions that maximize accumulated rewards over time. This chapter delves into the key concepts behind reinforcement learning, analyzing the relationship between the environment and the agent, and laying the groundwork for understanding how these elements interact in real-world situations.

Key Concepts

To understand reinforcement learning, it is essential to familiarize oneself with several fundamental concepts that are cornerstones of its functioning. One of the most important elements is the **agent**. This is the system that makes decisions within the environment. We can imagine an agent as a player in a game, a robot in a race, or even software that optimizes resource management. The agent acts based on what it observes, and its goal is to learn the best way to interact with the environment to receive the highest possible rewards.

The **environment**, in this context, refers to everything that the agent interacts with. It can include anything that influences the agent's decisions: the board in a chess game, a maze in a simulation, or even a set of conditions in an industrial control system. The definition of the environment is crucial as it determines the rules and constraints within which the agent must operate.

In the context of reinforcement learning, a state is a representation of the current situation of the environment in which the agent finds itself. For example, in a chess game, the state could be the arrangement of all the pieces on the board at a given moment. This representation of the state is fundamental because the agent uses this information to determine the best action to take.

An **action** is the specific decision made by the agent that affects the state of the environment. Continuing with the chess example, an action could be moving a piece to a new position on the board. Actions are the means by which the agent influences its environment and, consequently, receives feedback in the form of rewards.

The **reward** is crucial to the agent's learning. After taking an action, the agent receives a reward that can be positive or negative. This feedback acts as an incentive or disincentive, guiding the agent towards the actions that will maximize its success in the future. In the context of chess, capturing an opponent's piece could be considered a positive reward, while being checkmated would be a negative outcome.

For the agent to learn efficiently, it requires a **policy**, which defines the strategy it should follow in each state. The policy can be deterministic, where a single action is prescribed for each state, or stochastic, where a probability is assigned to each possible action. The policy is essential as it guides the agent's decision-making as it explores new strategies.

Finally, the **value function** is a metric that estimates the quality of an action in relation to the state in which the agent is. This function offers a long-term measure of the expected rewards. Understanding and optimizing the value function is essential for enabling the agent to develop effective strategies that maximize its total gain over time.

Environment and Agent

The interaction between the agent and the environment is at the core of reinforcement learning. At each time step, the agent observes the state of the environment, chooses an action according to its policy, and then receives a reward along with a new state of the environment as a result of its choice. This process can be conceptualized as a feedback loop. The agent is constantly seeking to improve its actions and, therefore, maximize the accumulated reward over time.

This cycle can be visualized tangibly with a simple example. Imagine a toy cart moving along a track. In this case, the cart is our agent and the track is the environment. The cart observes its current state on the track and, depending on its movement policy, decides to advance or turn. The action it takes will place it in a new position on the track, a new state. Depending on its new location, the cart may receive rewards; for example, getting closer to a goal or earning points for avoiding obstacles. As the cart continues navigating the track, it continuously adjusts, seeking to find the optimal combination of movements that will allow it to accumulate the most points.

This cycle of learning through exploration and exploitation is an essential aspect of reinforcement learning. Through its interactions with the environment, the agent gains a form of teaching that enables it to evaluate the success of different actions and adapt its policy accordingly. This transforms the agent's experience into knowledge, improving its ability to make informed decisions in the future.

Practical Example: Game Environment

To illustrate these concepts, let's consider a simple environment in the form of a maze game, where the agent's objective is to find the exit. This environment can be modeled with a matrix, where each cell represents a state. Each cell has its own set of conditions: some may be empty spaces (where the agent can move), while others may be walls (obstacles that the agent cannot pass through). Below is an example in Python that shows how this maze is defined:

```python
import numpy as np


# Define the maze where '0' represents a free space and '1'
represents a wall

maze = np.array([
    [0, 1, 0, 0, 0],
    [0, 1, 0, 1, 0],
    [0, 0, 0, 1, 0],
    [1, 1, 0, 0, 0],
    [0, 0, 0, 1, 0],
])

initial_state = (0, 0)  # Starting position of the agent
final_state = (4, 4)    # Target position
```

In this example, the agent will start at the initial state and will be provided with a set of possible actions, such as moving up, down, left, or right. The way the agent moves and interacts with the environment determines the state it arrives at. By moving into an empty space, the agent would receive a positive reward, while colliding with a wall would lead to a penalty. This type of environment allows the agent to directly experience the consequences of its actions and adjust accordingly.

Moreover, in a maze game like this, it might be useful to incorporate a reward system that favors not only exiting the maze but also the time taken to do so, encouraging the agent to find the quickest solution. This introduces complexity into the formulation of the policy, as the agent must balance the immediate reward of moving toward a safe space against the ultimate goal of efficiently exiting the maze.

Conclusion

Understanding the fundamentals of reinforcement learning is essential to explore the more advanced and complex techniques that will be developed in the following chapters. This chapter has established the key concepts and the dynamics between the agent and the environment, showing how this interaction can be modeled and utilized to solve problems. The foundations built here are vital for applying reinforcement learning in practical situations, where challenges range from altering behavior in a video game to optimizing systems in the real world. As we progress, we will delve into specific methods and applications that demonstrate the true potential of reinforcement learning, revealing a world rich in possibilities and discoveries.

## Chapter 3

Deep Q-Learning

Reinforcement learning has proven to be a powerful tool in the field of artificial intelligence, allowing agents to learn to make complex decisions through interaction with their environment. One of the most significant extensions of this approach is Deep Q-Learning, which combines classical reinforcement learning with deep neural networks. This chapter will explore basic Q-Learning, the implementation of Deep Q-Learning, and its practical use cases.

Basic Q-Learning

Q-Learning is an algorithm that enables an agent to learn to make decisions by interacting with an environment. Through experience, the agent updates a Q-value table (action values) that captures the expected value of actions in different states. These values are fundamental to guide the agent's decisions towards maximizing long-term rewards.

In the context of Q-Learning, the action-value function Q is denoted as $Q(s, a)$, where s is a state and a is an action. The main idea is that over time, the agent will learn to optimize its decisions to maximize the accumulated rewards.

The Bellman Equation

One of the foundations of Q-Learning is the Bellman equation, which establishes the relationship between the value of an action in a state and the expected rewards from its future actions. It is mathematically expressed as follows:

$$Q(s, a) \leftarrow Q(s, a) + \alpha\left(r + \gamma \max_{a'} Q(s', a') - Q(s, a)\right)$$

In this equation:

- α is the learning rate, which determines the extent to which new experiences influence the learned values.

- r is the immediate reward obtained after executing action a.

- γ is the discount factor, which determines the importance of future rewards compared to current rewards.

- s' is the new state in which the agent finds itself after executing action a.

The aim is for the agent to explore its environment and cover all possible combinations of states and actions, iteratively adjusting its Q-values using the Bellman equation.

Limitations of Classical Q-Learning

While classical Q-Learning is effective in simple environments, it presents significant limitations when dealing with large state and action spaces. For example, if an agent is learning to play a complex game, the Q-table can become unwieldy as it would require an entry for every combination of state and action. This is where Deep Q-Learning comes into play, utilizing neural networks to generalize and approximate this value function.

Implementation of Deep Q-Learning

Deep Q-Learning uses a deep neural network instead of a Q-table to estimate Q-values. This allows the agent to tackle problems with much larger and more complex state spaces. Below are the key components and steps involved in implementing Deep Q-Learning.

Neural Network Structure

The neural network used in Deep Q-Learning typically has the following architecture:

- **Input Layer**: Represents the current state of the environment. This can be an image (in the case of visual games) or a feature vector (in more abstract settings).

- **Hidden Layers**: These layers are responsible for processing information and learning useful representations of the environment. Usually, multiple hidden layers are used to allow the network to learn complex patterns.

- **Output Layer**: This layer produces Q-values for each possible action, given the features of the current state.

Training Process

The training infrastructure for Deep Q-Learning can be summarized in the following steps:

1. **Initialization**: The neural network is initialized, and an experience

memory is created to store transitions of state, action, reward, and next state.

2. **Interaction with the Environment**: The agent selects actions (explores or exploits) based on a policy that can be ε-greedy, where with probability ε it chooses a random action (exploration) and with probability $1 - \diamond$ it chooses the action with the highest Q-value (exploitation).

3. **Storing Experiences**: After executing an action, the agent stores the observed transition in the experience memory.

4. **Sampling Experiences**: A random set of experiences is sampled from memory. These experiences are used to train the neural network and update the parameters of the Q-function.

5. **Updating Through Backpropagation**: The loss between the Q-value estimated by the network and the target Q-value, calculated using the Bellman equation, is computed. The network is trained via backpropagation to minimize this loss.

6. **Repetition**: This process is repeated over multiple episodes until the agent learns optimal behavior.

Code Example: Deep Q-Learning

Below is a simplified example of a Deep Q-Learning agent training in a basic environment. We will use TensorFlow to build the neural network.

```
1  import numpy as np
2  import random
3  import tensorflow as tf
4  from collections import deque
5
6  class DQNAgent:
```

```python
    def __init__(self, state_size, action_size):
        self.state_size = state_size
        self.action_size = action_size
        self.memory = deque(maxlen=2000)
        self.gamma = 0.95  # discount factor
        self.epsilon = 1.0  # exploration rate
        self.epsilon_min = 0.01
        self.epsilon_decay = 0.995
        self.learning_rate = 0.001
        self.model = self._build_model()

    def _build_model(self):
        model = tf.keras.Sequential()
        model.add(tf.keras.layers.Dense(24, input_dim=self.
    state_size, activation='relu'))
        model.add(tf.keras.layers.Dense(24, activation=
    'relu'))
        model.add(tf.keras.layers.Dense(self.action_size,
    activation='linear'))
        model.compile(loss='mse', optimizer=tf.keras.
    optimizers.Adam(lr=self.learning_rate))
        return model

    def remember(self, state, action, reward, next_state,
    done):
        self.memory.append((state, action, reward,
    next_state, done))

    def act(self, state):
        if np.random.rand() <= self.epsilon:
            return random.randrange(self.action_size)
        act_values = self.model.predict(state)
        return np.argmax(act_values[0])
    # returns the action with the highest Q-value

```

```
35     def replay(self, batch_size):
36         minibatch = random.sample(self.memory, batch_size)
37         for state, action, reward, next_state, done in
   minibatch:
38             target = reward
39             if not done:
40                 target += self.gamma * np.amax(self.model.
   predict(next_state)[0])
41             target_f = self.model.predict(state)
42             target_f[0][action] = target
43             self.model.fit(state, target_f, epochs=1,
   verbose=0)
44         if self.epsilon > self.epsilon_min:
45             self.epsilon *= self.epsilon_decay
```

In this example, a `DQNAgent` class is defined that encapsulates the behavior and properties of an agent using Deep Q-Learning. This agent can remember transitions, select actions, and update its neural network model based on experience.

Use Cases

Deep Q-Learning has been utilized in a variety of practical applications that have demonstrated its effectiveness. Some notable cases include:

- **Video Games**: One of the most recognized examples of Deep Q-Learning is the victory of trained agents over the classic Atari game, such as "Breakout". In this context, agents used computer vision to determine the state and learn to play, surpassing humans in their respective tasks.

- **Robotics**: In the field of robotics, Deep Q-Learning has been used to teach robots to navigate complex environments and perform specific tasks, such as object manipulation, where precise and quick decisions are critical.

- **System Control**: Deep Q-Learning approaches have also been explored in system control, such as dynamic parameter tuning in industrial systems, where agents optimize performance under changing conditions.

Conclusion

Deep Q-Learning has expanded the possibilities of reinforcement learning, allowing agents to learn in much more complex and challenging environments. Its ability to effectively combine exploration and exploitation, supported by deep neural networks, has exceeded expectations in terms of performance. Throughout this chapter, we have explored the key concepts of basic Q-Learning, the implementation of Deep Q-Learning, and some use cases that illustrate its power in various contexts. In the upcoming chapters, we will continue to delve into other advanced techniques that further expand the horizons of the field of artificial intelligence.

## Chapter 4

Introduction to Generative Models

In the field of artificial intelligence, generative models have gained significant importance as they allow not only the classification and extraction of information from data but also the creation of new samples that have a realistic and coherent appearance. This chapter focuses on defining what generative models are, their applications, and how they work in practice, opening the door to impactful technological innovations across various areas.

Definition and Applications

A generative model is a system capable of learning the underlying distribution of a dataset to subsequently generate new data that follows the same distribution. This contrasts with discriminative models, which focus solely on the classification of existing data. Generative models are used in a variety of applications, such as:

- **Image Generation**: The creation of new images from a training dataset. This includes applications in generative art, product design, fashion, and more.

- **Voice Synthesis**: Models that generate audio from text, enabling the creation of virtual assistants that speak naturally.

- **Text Generation**: Systems that create coherent text, such as automatic summaries, stories, or responses in a conversational dialogue.

- **Completion of Missing Data**: Where it can fill in missing values or complete images in areas with missing information, playing a crucial role in data preprocessing.

This variety of applications shows how generative models can function as versatile tools in the creation and manipulation of data.

How Generative Models Work

The essence of a generative model is its ability to learn from an existing dataset, modeling its distribution. This can be achieved through various methodologies and approaches, which often involve advanced machine learning algorithms. Below are some of the most commonly used approaches to build generative models.

1. Statistical Models

Statistical approaches are some of the oldest and simplest in developing generative models. A common example is the use of probability distributions, where a function is fitted to observed data. For example, a Gaussian mixture is a generative model that is used to model the distribution of data believed to come from several underlying Gaussian distributions.

2. Generative Neural Networks

In the modern era of AI, neural networks have revolutionized the field of generative models. Two of the most prominent approaches in this area are Generative Adversarial Networks (GANs) and Variational Autoencoders (VAEs).

Generative Adversarial Networks (GANs)

GANs, introduced by Ian Goodfellow in 2014, consist of two neural networks: the generator and the discriminator. These networks compete against each other in a game framework:

- **Generator**: Its goal is to create images (or data) that are indistinguishable from real data.

- **Discriminator**: Its job is to differentiate between real images and those generated by the generator.

This approach resembles a game of "cat and mouse," where the generator continuously improves to fool the discriminator. The competitive dynamic between both networks drives improvements in the quality of generated samples.

Variational Autoencoders (VAEs)

VAEs are another powerful approach for data generation. They are designed to learn the latent representation of data in a compressed space. The process involves two parts:

- **Encoder**: Compresses the input data into a latent space, extracting meaningful features.

- **Decoder**: Uses these latent representations to reconstruct data that resembles the original data.

Through a combination of variability techniques and information recovery, VAEs can create new data that possesses realistic variations.

Application Example: Image Generation with GANs

To illustrate the practical functioning of generative models, we will analyze an example that uses GANs for image creation. Suppose we want to train a generator that creates images of human faces. Here, the basic workflow would involve the following steps:

1. Data Collection: We gather a set of images of human faces, for example, from a public dataset like CelebA.

2. Network Design: We build the GAN model with a generator and a discriminator. Below is a basic example of how the code might look in Python using TensorFlow:

```python
import tensorflow as tf
from tensorflow.keras import layers

def build_generator(latent_dim):
    model = tf.keras.Sequential()
    model.add(layers.Dense(128, activation='relu',
    input_dim=latent_dim))
    model.add(layers.BatchNormalization())
    model.add(layers.Dense(256, activation='relu'))
    model.add(layers.BatchNormalization())
    model.add(layers.Dense(512, activation='relu'))
    model.add(layers.BatchNormalization())
    model.add(layers.Dense(1024, activation='relu'))
```

```
13      model.add(layers.BatchNormalization())
14      model.add(layers.Dense(28 * 28 * 1, activation='tanh'))
15      model.add(layers.Reshape((28, 28, 1)))
16      return model
17
18  def build_discriminator():
19      model = tf.keras.Sequential()
20      model.add(layers.Flatten(input_shape=(28, 28, 1)))
21      model.add(layers.Dense(512, activation='relu'))
22      model.add(layers.Dropout(0.3))
23      model.add(layers.Dense(256, activation='relu'))
24      model.add(layers.Dropout(0.3))
25      model.add(layers.Dense(1, activation='sigmoid'))
26      return model
27
28  latent_dim = 100
29  generator = build_generator(latent_dim)
30  discriminator = build_discriminator()
```

3. Training: We train both networks in a loop where the generator tries to fool the discriminator with fake images while the discriminator strives to identify real images. This process is repeated in each epoch.

4. Generation of New Images: Once the model is trained, we can generate new images simply by feeding random noise into the generator.

```
1  import numpy as np
2  import matplotlib.pyplot as plt
3
4  # Generate images
5  noise = np.random.normal(0, 1, (10, latent_dim))
6  generated_images = generator.predict(noise)
7
8  # Display generated images
```

```
 9  for i in range(10):
10      plt.subplot(2, 5, i + 1)
11      plt.imshow(generated_images[i, :, :, 0], cmap='gray')
12      plt.axis('off')
13  plt.show()
```

This simple workflow demonstrates how, by implementing and training a GAN model, images of faces can be created that at first glance seem genuine.

Challenges in Generative Models

Although generative models have proven effective, they face several challenges:

- **Mode Collapse**: A situation where the generator produces a limited set of outputs that might be indistinguishable to the discriminator, depriving the model of its ability to generate diversity.

- **Data Quality**: The quality and diversity of training data are essential. If the data is biased or unrepresentative, the generated samples will reflect those biases.

- **Result Evaluation**: Defining effective metrics to assess the quality of generated samples is a complicated aspect, as there is often no "correct answer."

Conclusion

Generative models are a fundamental part of the artificial intelligence ecosystem, with enormous potential spanning various applications. As technology and approaches continue to evolve, new opportunities and challenges are emerging in this area. Understanding how these models work, their fundamentals, and their applications is crucial for anyone looking to make significant contributions in the field of AI. Throughout this chapter, we have explored the basic principles behind generative models, providing a glimpse into their internal workings and the exciting possibilities they can open for the future.

## Chapter 5

Generative Adversarial Networks (GANs)

Generative Adversarial Networks (GANs) have taken center stage in the field of artificial intelligence, challenging the norms of digital content generation. Introduced by Ian Goodfellow and his team in 2014, GANs allow models not only to learn from data but also to create new samples that are indistinguishable from real samples. This chapter explores the architecture of GANs, their functioning, varieties, applications, and challenges associated with this innovative approach.

Architecture and Functioning

The fundamental concept behind GANs is the idea of a confrontation between two neural networks that compete against each other: the **generator** and the **discriminator**. This dynamic resembles a game, where the generator tries to produce data that deceives the discriminator, and the discriminator tries to improve its ability to distinguish between real and generated data.

Generator

The generator is responsible for creating fake data from a random noise vector. It can be conceptualized as an artist trying to create a painting that resembles a masterpiece. The task of the generator is to learn what the "style" and "structure" of the real data are and use that information to create new data that is as close to reality as possible.

Symbolic Example: Imagine an artist who observes various artworks to learn how to create a particular painting. Each time he creates a new painting (generated data), he seeks to improve it based on previous results, just as the generator does in a GAN.

Discriminator

The role of the discriminator is to be the art critic. Its goal is to evaluate whether the painting is real or generated. By learning to identify subtle differences between true and generated data, the discriminator becomes more skilled at spotting the authentic versus the fictitious.

Symbolic Example: The art critic has learned about specific characteristics from great masters, developing a keen eye to notice what elements are missing in the works of students.

Training Process

During training, the generator and discriminator improve together, following these steps:

1. **Discriminator Training**: The discriminator is presented with a collection of real data along with some samples generated by the

generator. Its task is to correctly classify the data as real or fake.

2. **Generator Training**: The generator then produces a new batch of data. Next, the discriminator is asked to evaluate this new data. The goal of the generator is to maximize the discriminator's error rate, meaning that the discriminator classifies its generated data as real.

3. **Feedback**: Through feedback, the generator adjusts its parameters to improve in its task, while the discriminator does the same to become more accurate.

The optimization process continues over multiple iterations until an equilibrium is reached, where the generator produces credible samples and the discriminator becomes more efficient in its discernment task.

Varieties of GANs

Since the introduction of the basic architecture of GANs, multiple variants have been developed to tackle different challenges or specific areas. Some of the most notable variants include:

Conditional GANs (cGANs)

Conditional GANs allow control over the type of generated data by adding additional information to the generator. For example, if images of clothing for different types are desired, inputs to the generator can be conditioned with labels indicating the desired type of garment.

Example: By providing the label "shoes" to the generator, the model will create images that represent only shoes, instead of a random mix of items.

Progressive Growing GANs

This approach allows training to occur at a low resolution and gradually increase. As the model trains, layers are added to the network, enabling more effective generation of high-resolution images. This technique has proven successful in creating complex and detailed images, such as human faces.

Symbolic Example: Imagine a photographer starting by taking low-resolution photos and, as they gain skill, increase the quality and detail of their shots, making each subsequent step more precise.

StyleGAN

Developed by NVIDIA, StyleGAN is famous for its ability to generate human faces that look surprisingly real. It employs a style-based approach that allows granular control over specific features of the generated data, such as hairstyle or facial expression.

This approach has revolutionized the concept of generating high-quality images, allowing for intuitive and advanced manipulation of human features.

Symbolic Example: Similar to a fashion designer who can adjust every little detail of an outfit, StyleGAN allows the adjustment of specifications in the creation of faces.

CycleGAN

CycleGAN is another variant that allows conversion between two domains of images (for example, converting horse images into zebra images and vice versa) without needing directly related training pairs. Through a feedback cycle, CycleGAN learns to perform style transfers while retaining important features of each domain.

Example: Think of a painter who can reproduce any painting in their own style; they don't need to have the original in sight, just understanding the essence of it.

Applications of GANs

The flexibility and capability of GANs have allowed their implementation in various real-world applications. Some of these applications include:

- **Image Generation**: Creating faces, animals, and scenes that are indistinguishable from real images. From academic applications to advertising, these generated images are widely used.

- **Image Enhancement**: Projects like super-resolution image generation where GANs improve the quality of low-resolution images.

- **Artistic Outcomes**: Generating new and experimental visual art, where GANs create original works that emulate the style of famous artists.

- **Cybersecurity**: Generating synthetic data for training models, minimizing the risk of data leaks and ensuring user privacy.

- **Simulation and Modeling**: In areas such as automotive, GANs are used to generate synthetic data for training in autonomous driving simulations.

Challenges and Considerations

Despite the promise of GANs, there are several challenges and ethical considerations worth discussing:

- **Mode Collapse**: Sometimes, the generator finds a small set of samples that deceive the discriminator, leading to a lack of diversity in the generated data. This results in the model producing the same images repeatedly.

- **Ethics and Misuse**: The power of GANs to create extremely realistic images raises ethical concerns, especially in the context of creating misleading or false content. The possibility of using generated images for impersonation or disinformation is a significant risk.

- **Quality Evaluation**: Evaluating the quality of generated images remains a challenge. The absence of universal metrics can complicate the validation process, and robust methods for classifying and evaluating generated samples need to be developed.

Conclusion

Generative Adversarial Networks are a significant achievement at the intersection of artificial intelligence and creativity. Their ability to learn and generate new data opens a world of opportunities, not only in the artistic realm but across various application areas. As technology continues to evolve, it is vital to address challenges and ethical concerns to ensure these tools are used responsibly and effectively. Understanding GANs is essential not only for researchers but also for anyone interested in the future of artificial intelligence and digital content generation.

## Chapter 6

Variational Autoencoders (VAEs)

Variational Autoencoders (VAEs) have emerged as one of the most effective tools for data generation in the field of artificial intelligence. Through their capacity to learn latent representations of the data, VAEs not only offer a means of data compression, but also allow for the generation of new samples that maintain characteristics consistent with the training dataset. In this chapter, we will explore the basic functioning of VAEs, their architecture, comparisons with other generative models such as GANs, and their practical applications.

Basic Functioning of VAEs

VAEs are structured around the idea that each input data point can be represented as a combination of hidden latent features. Instead of trying to directly reconstruct the original data, a VAE seeks to learn a probability distribution over these latent representations.

Encoder and Decoder

The architecture of a VAE consists of two main parts: the **encoder** and the **decoder**.

- **Encoder**: Its goal is to take an input data point and map it to a latent space, defined by mean and variance parameters. This process is based on variational inference, where the encoder is trained to approximate the posterior $p(z \mid x)$, where z are the latent variables and x is the input data. Instead of producing a single latent value, the encoder produces mean and variance vectors that are used to construct a multivariate normal distribution in the latent space.

- **Decoder**: The main task of the decoder is to reconstruct the original data from a sample taken from the latent distribution. Thus, in the case of a VAE, the decoder seeks to model the probability distribution $p(x \mid z)$ to generate data from the latent variables.

The Cost Equation

Training a VAE is based on maximizing the **marginal likelihood** of the model, which involves two key components: the reconstruction of the original data and the regularization of the latent distribution. This process is formalized in the cost function, which is defined as the sum of the reconstruction loss and the Kullback-Leibler (KL) divergence between the latent distribution and a standard normal distribution:

$$L = E_{q(z \mid x)}[\log p(x \mid z)] - D_{KL}(q(z \mid x) \| p(z))$$

Where D_{KL} measures how different the encoder's approximated distribution $q(z \mid x)$ is from the prior distribution $p(z)$.

Comparison between VAEs and GANs

Although VAEs and GANs are two of the most prominent generative models, they exhibit some key differences in their approach and functioning.

Generation Objective

- **VAEs**: Focus on learning a continuous latent representation and on the reconstruction of the original data. By integrating the regularization of the latent distribution, they ensure that the generated samples are coherent and diverse.

- **GANs**: Utilize a competitive approach between a generator and a discriminator, where the generator learns to produce samples that deceive the discriminator. This process can lead to a lack of diversity (mode collapse) compared to the VAE approach.

Interpretability

- **VAEs**: The generativity and structure of the latent space tend to be more interpretable, as they allow for probabilistic inferences and a clearer understanding of how the data relates. For example, interpolation between different points in the latent space translates into smooth variations between the generated samples.

- **GANs**: While they can generate high-quality and realistic results, they are often more difficult to interpret due to their competitive nature.

Implementation Example: Variational Autoencoder

To illustrate how VAEs work, below is a basic implementation of a VAE in Python using TensorFlow.

Importing Libraries

First, let's make sure to have the necessary libraries installed. You might need to install them with `pip` if they are not already available in your environment.

```
1  pip install tensorflow numpy matplotlib
```

VAE Code

Here is the code for a simple VAE to generate digit images from the MNIST dataset:

```
1  import numpy as np
2  import matplotlib.pyplot as plt
3  import tensorflow as tf
4  from tensorflow.keras import layers, models
5
6
   # Define the size of the images and the size of the latent
   space

7  img_size = 28 * 28
```

```python
8   latent_dim = 2
9
10  # Encoder
11  def build_encoder():
12      inputs = layers.Input(shape=(img_size,))
13      h = layers.Dense(512, activation='relu')(inputs)
14      z_mean = layers.Dense(latent_dim)(h)
15      z_log_var = layers.Dense(latent_dim)(h)
16
17      def sampling(args):
18          z_mean, z_log_var = args
19          epsilon = tf.keras.backend.random_normal(shape=(tf.
    shape(z_mean)[0], latent_dim))
20          return z_mean + tf.exp(0.5 * z_log_var) * epsilon
21
22      z = layers.Lambda(sampling, output_shape=(latent_dim,))
    ([z_mean, z_log_var])
23      return models.Model(inputs, [z_mean, z_log_var, z],
    name="encoder")
24
25  # Decoder
26  def build_decoder():
27      latent_inputs = layers.Input(shape=(latent_dim,))
28      h = layers.Dense(512, activation='relu')(latent_inputs)
29      outputs = layers.Dense(img_size, activation='sigmoid')(
    h)
30      return models.Model(latent_inputs, outputs, name=
    "decoder")
31
32  # Build and compile the VAE
33  encoder = build_encoder()
34  decoder = build_decoder()
35
36  inputs = layers.Input(shape=(img_size,))
37  z_mean, z_log_var, z = encoder(inputs)
```

```python
38   outputs = decoder(z)
39
40   vae = models.Model(inputs, outputs)
41   vae.compile(optimizer='adam', loss='binary_crossentropy')
42
43   # Training the VAE
44   # Load the MNIST dataset
45   (x_train, _), (x_test, _) = tf.keras.datasets.mnist.
     load_data()
46   x_train = x_train.reshape(-1, img_size) / 255.0
47   x_test = x_test.reshape(-1, img_size) / 255.0
48
49   # Train the model
50   vae.fit(x_train, x_train, epochs=30, batch_size=128)
51
52   # Generate new images
53   def plot_generated_images(model, n=10):
54       z_sample = np.random.normal(size=(n, latent_dim))
55       generated_images = model.predict(z_sample)
56       generated_images = generated_images.reshape(-1, 28, 28)
57
58       for i in range(n):
59           plt.subplot(2, 5, i + 1)
60           plt.imshow(generated_images[i], cmap='gray')
61           plt.axis('off')
62       plt.show()
63
64   plot_generated_images(decoder)
```

Code Description

1. **Encoder and Decoder**: The functions `build_encoder` and `build_decoder` are defined to create the subnets of the VAE. The encoder produces a mean and a log-variance, while the

decoder takes the latent variable to reconstruct the image.

2. **VAE Model**: The complete model consists of the encoder and the decoder, where the decoder's output is used to calculate the loss during training.

3. **Training**: The model is trained using the MNIST dataset, a collection of images of handwritten digits. The data is normalized and used for training the model.

4. **Image Generation**: After training, new images are generated by taking random samples from the latent space, demonstrating how the model can create new digits.

Practical Applications of VAEs

VAEs have found a wide range of applications in various areas, including:

- **Image Generation**: Creating new designs, art, or photographic images for entertainment, product design, or fashion.

- **Text Synthesis**: VAEs can be used to generate text similarly to how they generate images, by learning linguistic and syntactic representations.

- **Data Compression**: By learning latent representations, VAEs can be employed to effectively reduce the dimensionality of data, facilitating storage and transmission processes.

- **Imputation of Missing Data**: In scenarios where there are missing values in datasets, VAEs can learn to impute these values, maintaining the consistency of the model.

Final Considerations

Variational Autoencoders represent a significant evolution in the field of data generation. Their capacity to learn latent representations and produce new examples from them has made them an essential component of modern artificial intelligence. As research advances, it is exciting to contemplate the future of VAEs and their potential impact across various industries. With their foundation in probabilistic inference and computational structure, VAEs continue to challenge and expand the boundaries of digital content generation.

## Chapter 7

Autoencoders

Autoencoders are a family of unsupervised learning models that have gained popularity in the field of artificial intelligence, especially in data generation and compression. An autoencoder's ability to learn efficient and compact representations of a dataset makes it a powerful tool across a variety of applications, from dimensionality reduction to synthetic data generation. This chapter delves into the structure and functioning of autoencoders, their variations, practical applications, and associated challenges.

Structure and Functioning of Autoencoders

An autoencoder consists of two main parts: the **encoder** and the **decoder**. This structure allows the model to learn to represent data in a lower-dimensional space and then reconstruct it from that representation.

Encoder

The encoder is the first part of the autoencoder, tasked with taking an input and converting it into a more compact latent representation. This process involves dimensionality reduction, where the model extracts the most relevant and significant features from the dataset. Internally, the encoder typically consists of a series of neural layers that transform the original input into a compressed space.

A good example to understand the encoder is to imagine a company that possesses a large amount of customer data, including details like name, address, purchase history, among others. If the company wants to analyze purchasing patterns, it could waste time looking at a large number of variables. Instead, the encoder "condenses" all that information into a single feature vector that adequately represents customer behavior.

Decoder

The decoder is the second part of the autoencoder, and its purpose is to take the latent representation generated by the encoder and reconstruct the original input. The goal here is for the decoder's output to be as similar as possible to the initial input, which implies that the model has learned to extract the most relevant features. If the encoder acts as a compressor, the decoder acts as a decompressor.

Returning to the example of the company, the decoder would attempt to reconstruct all the customer details from that compressed vector. This enables the company not only to recover complete data but also to assess which customer features are the most influential in their purchasing decisions.

Training Process

Training an autoencoder involves minimizing the difference between the original input and the reconstructed output. To achieve this, the **loss** function is used, which measures the error in reconstruction. This process can be formalized with the following equation:

$$\text{Loss} = \frac{1}{N} \sum_{i=1}^{N} \left|\left| x_i - \hat{x}_i \right|\right|^2$$

where x_i is the original input, $\hat{x}_i$ is the reconstructed output, and N is the total number of inputs.

The autoencoder is trained with the goal of minimizing this loss function using optimization algorithms like gradient descent. As it trains, the model adjusts the parameters of the neural layers to improve the quality of the reconstruction.

Types of Autoencoders

There are several variations of autoencoders, each designed to address different problems and requirements. Below are some of the most common.

Denoising Autoencoders

Denoising autoencoders are designed to learn to reconstruct the input from intentionally degraded data. In this case, during training, the model receives an input that has been altered (for example, by adding noise) and must learn to reconstruct the "clean" version of the original input. This is reminiscent of how humans can recognize objects in a noisy environment by learning to ignore irrelevant details.

Example

Imagine a photographer faced with an image distorted or noisy due to poor lighting conditions. A denoising autoencoder can help clean the image by restoring it to its original form by learning patterns that define the relevant parts of the image.

Sparse Autoencoders

Sparse autoencoders introduce a sparsity constraint in the encoding process. This means that the encoder tries to have a limited number of active units in its latent representation, allowing the network to learn more robust and relevant features. The sparsity regularization can be achieved by adding a penalty term to the loss function.

Variational Autoencoders (VAEs)

Variational autoencoders (VAEs) are mentioned in a previous chapter, but it is important to note that they present key differences from traditional autoencoders. VAEs focus on probabilistic inference, while classical autoencoders directly optimize the loss function without considering the distribution of latent representations.

Convolutional Autoencoders

Convolutional autoencoders use convolutional layers in their architecture, making them particularly effective for working with image data. This type of autoencoder can capture important spatial features through convolutions, resulting in more efficient representations for image reconstruction.

Applications of Autoencoders

Autoencoders have multiple practical applications in various areas. Some of the most notable include:

Dimensionality Reduction

Autoencoders are used to reduce the dimensionality of large and complex datasets, offering an alternative to traditional methods like PCA (Principal Component Analysis). By transforming the original data into a more compact space, data analysis and visualization can be facilitated.

Anomaly Detection

Autoencoders are effective in detecting anomalies in data. By training an autoencoder on a dataset where the samples are mostly "normal," any input that produces a high reconstruction error can be considered anomalous. This is useful in applications like monitoring product quality on a production line or detecting fraud in financial transactions.

Synthetic Data Generation

As mentioned earlier, autoencoders can be used to generate synthetic examples of data. This is especially useful in scenarios where data is scarce or difficult to obtain.

Missing Data Imputation

Autoencoders can learn to fill in missing data in a dataset, using the information available from other variables to predict missing values.

Example Implementation: Autoencoder in Python

Below is a simple implementation example of an autoencoder using Python and TensorFlow. This model will be trained to learn to reconstruct images from the MNIST dataset.

Importing Libraries

First, we need to install and ensure we have the necessary libraries:

```
1  pip install tensorflow numpy matplotlib
```

Autoencoder Code

Here is the code for a basic autoencoder:

```
1  import numpy as np
2  import matplotlib.pyplot as plt
3  import tensorflow as tf
4  from tensorflow.keras import layers, models
5
6  # Load the MNIST dataset
7  (x_train, _), (x_test, _) = tf.keras.datasets.mnist.
   load_data()
8  x_train = x_train.reshape(-1, 28 * 28) / 255.0
   # Normalization
```

```python
 9  x_test = x_test.reshape(-1, 28 * 28) / 255.0
    # Normalization
10
11  # Define the architecture of the Autoencoder
12  input_img = layers.Input(shape=(28 * 28,))
13  encoded = layers.Dense(128, activation='relu')(input_img)
14  decoded = layers.Dense(28 * 28, activation='sigmoid')(
    encoded)
15
16  autoencoder = models.Model(input_img, decoded)
17
18  # Now define the "encoder" separately
19  encoder_model = models.Model(input_img, encoded)
20
21  # Compile the autoencoder
22  autoencoder.compile(optimizer='adam', loss=
    'binary_crossentropy')
23
24  # Train the model
25  autoencoder.fit(x_train, x_train, epochs=50, batch_size=256
    , validation_data=(x_test, x_test))
26
27  # Generate new images to evaluate the reconstruction
28  decoded_imgs = autoencoder.predict(x_test)
29
30  # Display some original images and their reconstructions
31  n = 10  # Number of images to show
32  plt.figure(figsize=(20, 4))
33  for i in range(n):
34      # Original
35      ax = plt.subplot(2, n, i + 1)
36      plt.imshow(x_test[i].reshape(28, 28), cmap='gray')
37      plt.axis('off')
38
39      # Reconstruction
```

```
40      ax = plt.subplot(2, n, i + 1 + n)
41      plt.imshow(decoded_imgs[i].reshape(28, 28), cmap='gray'
)
42      plt.axis('off')
43  plt.show()
```

Summary of the Code

1. **Load and Preprocess Data**: We load the MNIST dataset and normalize the pixel values, ensuring that the images are in a range of [0, 1].

2. **Define the Architecture of the Autoencoder**: Dense layers are created for both the encoder and the decoder. The encoder reduces the dimensionality to 128 neurons, while the decoder restores it to the original dimensionality.

3. **Compilation and Training**: The model is compiled and trained using the dataset, minimizing reconstruction loss.

4. **Evaluation of Results**: We generate new images from the test images and compare the original images with the reconstructed ones, displaying the results to assess the effectiveness of the autoencoder.

Challenges and Considerations

Despite their effectiveness, autoencoders present certain challenges. One of the main issues is **overfitting**, where the model adapts too closely to the training data and fails to generalize to new data. To mitigate this, techniques such as regularization or dropout can be employed.

Furthermore, while autoencoders are useful for unsupervised learning, they can sometimes lack the capacity to create representations as complex and realistic as those obtained from more advanced generative models, such as GANs or VAEs.

Conclusion

Autoencoders are powerful and versatile tools in the field of artificial intelligence. Their architecture, composed of an encoder and a decoder, facilitates the compression and reconstruction of data, and their ability to learn efficient representations makes them applicable in a wide variety of scenarios. As research advances and new variants emerge, autoencoders continue to challenge conventions in data generation, providing innovative solutions to complex problems.

## Chapter 8

Advanced Dimensionality Reduction

Dimensionality reduction is an essential technique in the field of artificial intelligence and data analysis. In situations where datasets contain a large number of variables, complexity can increase exponentially, leading to overfitting problems and increased processing time. In this chapter, we will address the relevant techniques and algorithms for advanced dimensionality reduction, as well as their practical applications in data analysis.

Fundamental Concepts

Dimensionality reduction refers to the process of reducing the number of random variables under consideration while seeking to preserve the most relevant information possible. This process is important for several reasons:

- **Visualization**: Facilitates the visualization of high-dimensional data in lower-dimensional spaces (e.g., 2D or 3D).

- **Noise Elimination**: Helps to remove noise and redundancy in the data.

- **Model Performance Improvement**: By reducing model complexity, the possibility of overfitting is decreased and generalization is improved.

The reduction process often involves transforming the dataset into a new space where the features are more significant and relevant. Below are some of the most important techniques in dimensionality reduction.

Principal Component Analysis (PCA)

Principal Component Analysis (PCA) is one of the most popular and widely used techniques for dimensionality reduction. PCA seeks to identify the directions in which there is the most variance in the data and project the data in those directions, known as principal components.

How PCA Works

PCA can be summarized in the following steps:

1. **Standardize the Data**: Ensure that each feature has a mean of zero and a variance of one, which allows all features to be comparable.

2. **Calculate the Covariance Matrix**: This matrix captures the relationship between variables. A high covariance value indicates that the variables are correlated.

3. **Calculate Eigenvalues and Eigenvectors**: By calculating the eigenvalues and eigenvectors of the covariance matrix, we can identify the directions in which the data is most spread out.

4. **Select Principal Components**: Choose the first k eigenvectors, where k is the number of dimensions we want to keep.

5. **Project the Data**: The original data is projected into the space defined by the first k eigenvectors.

PCA Example in Python

Let's see how to implement PCA in a practical context using Python and the scikit-learn library:

```python
1  import numpy as np
2  import matplotlib.pyplot as plt
3  from sklearn.decomposition import PCA
4  from sklearn.datasets import load_iris
5
6  # Load the iris dataset
7  data = load_iris()
8  X = data.data
9  y = data.target
10
11 # Apply PCA
12 pca = PCA(n_components=2)  # Reduce to 2 dimensions
13 X_reduced = pca.fit_transform(X)
14
15 # Visualize the reduction
16 plt.figure(figsize=(8, 6))
17 scatter = plt.scatter(X_reduced[:, 0], X_reduced[:, 1], c=y
   , cmap='viridis')
18 plt.xlabel('Principal Component 1')
19 plt.ylabel('Principal Component 2')
20 plt.title(
      'Principal Component Analysis on the Iris Dataset')
21 plt.legend(*scatter.legend_elements(), title='Classes')
```

```
22  plt.grid()
23  plt.show()
```

In this example, we applied PCA to the famous iris dataset, which contains features of various flower species. After reducing the dimensionality to two, we visualize the classes in a scatter plot.

t-Distributed Stochastic Neighbor Embedding (t-SNE)

While PCA focuses on linear variance, t-SNE is a non-linear technique used for dimensionality reduction, especially effective for visualizing high-dimensional data. t-SNE is very popular in the field of machine learning, particularly in classification problems and pattern identification.

How t-SNE Works

t-SNE follows these steps:

1. **Convert Distances to Probabilities**: For each point in the high-dimensional space, evaluate the distances to other points and convert those distances into probabilities using a Gaussian distribution. This creates a probabilistic representation of the similarity between points.

2. **Create a Distribution in the Low-Dimensional Space**: In the lower-dimensional space, points are distributed similarly using a Student's t probability distribution.

3. **Minimize Kullback-Leibler Divergence**: Optimize the distribution in the lower-dimensional space to resemble the distribution in the high-dimensional space, minimizing the Kullback-Leibler

divergence between the two distributions.

t-SNE Example in Python

Let's see a practical example of t-SNE using a more complex dataset:

```python
1   from sklearn.manifold import TSNE
2   from sklearn.datasets import load_digits
3
4   # Load the digits dataset
5   digits = load_digits()
6   X = digits.data
7   y = digits.target
8
9   # Apply t-SNE
10  tsne = TSNE(n_components=2, random_state=42)
11  X_tsne = tsne.fit_transform(X)
12
13  # Visualize the reduction
14  plt.figure(figsize=(8, 6))
15  scatter = plt.scatter(X_tsne[:, 0], X_tsne[:, 1], c=y, cmap='jet', alpha=0.5)
16  plt.xlabel('Dimension 1')
17  plt.ylabel('Dimension 2')
18  plt.title('Dimensionality Reduction using t-SNE')
19  plt.legend(*scatter.legend_elements(), title='Classes')
20  plt.grid()
21  plt.show()
```

This code applies t-SNE to the handwritten digits dataset, creating a plot that shows how different digits cluster together in the lower-dimensional space.

Correspondence Analysis

Correspondence Analysis is a technique especially useful for categorical data. While it resembles PCA, the approach used for categorical data is different, allowing for a visual representation of relationships between categories.

How Correspondence Analysis Works

1. **Construct a Contingency Table**: Start by creating a table that shows the frequency of categories.

2. **Calculate Correspondences**: This table is transformed to study the relationships between rows and columns.

3. **Project into a Lower-Dimensional Space**: Like PCA, the data is projected into a lower-dimensional space.

Correspondence Analysis Example in Python

Below is how to perform Correspondence Analysis using a fictional dataset:

```
import pandas as pd
from prince import MCA

# Create a fictional dataset
data = pd.DataFrame({
    'Animal': ['Cat', 'Dog', 'Bird', 'Cat', 'Bird', 'Dog',
'Bird', 'Cat'],
    'Color': ['Black', 'Brown', 'Black', 'White', 'Green',
'Brown', 'White', 'Black']
```

```
 8  })
 9
10  # Perform correspondence analysis
11  mca = MCA(n_components=2)
12  mca = mca.fit(data)
13
14  # Transform the data
15  transformed_data = mca.transform(data)
16
17  # Visualize the results
18  plt.figure(figsize=(8, 6))
19  plt.scatter(transformed_data[0], transformed_data[1], alpha
    =0.5)
20  plt.title(
    'Correspondence Analysis: Projection of Animals and Colors'
    )
21  plt.xlabel('Dimension 1')
22  plt.ylabel('Dimension 2')
23  plt.grid()
24  plt.show()
```

This example uses a simple dataset of animals and colors, allowing us to visualize how the categories relate to one another in a reduced space.

Autoencoders for Dimensionality Reduction

Autoencoders, which were discussed earlier, are another popular option for dimensionality reduction. By learning a latent representation of the data, they can capture non-linear and complex features that other techniques may overlook.

How Autoencoders Work

An autoencoder is trained to minimize the difference between the input and the output. By doing this, it can effectively compress and reconstruct the data. This latent representation can be used for dimension reduction.

Autoencoder Example for Dimensionality Reduction

Using the same digits dataset, let's see how to implement an autoencoder for dimensionality reduction:

```python
from tensorflow.keras import layers, models

# Define the Autoencoder architecture
input_img = layers.Input(shape=(64,))
# 64 is the flattened size of the digit images
encoded = layers.Dense(32, activation='relu')(input_img)
# Latent node of 32 dimensions
decoded = layers.Dense(64, activation='sigmoid')(encoded)
# Reconstruction

autoencoder = models.Model(input_img, decoded)

# Compile the autoencoder
autoencoder.compile(optimizer='adam', loss=
'binary_crossentropy')

# Train the model on the digits dataset
autoencoder.fit(X, X, epochs=50, batch_size=256)

# Dimensionality Reduction
encoder = models.Model(input_img, encoded)
X_encoded = encoder.predict(X)
```

```
19
20  # Visualize the result
21  plt.figure(figsize=(8, 6))
22  plt.scatter(X_encoded[:, 0], X_encoded[:, 1])
23  plt.title('Dimensionality Reduction using Autoencoders')
24  plt.xlabel('Component 1')
25  plt.ylabel('Component 2')
26  plt.grid()
27  plt.show()
```

Here, we observe how an autoencoder allows us to reduce the dimensional space and prepares the ground for subsequent analysis or classification.

Conclusions

Dimensionality reduction is a crucial tool in data processing and analysis. Throughout this chapter, we have explored several advanced techniques, each with its own advantages and disadvantages. From PCA, which is easy to implement and understand, to t-SNE, which offers rich visualizations of complex data, the selection of the appropriate technique will depend on the type of data and the specific objectives of the analysis.

The effectiveness of these techniques demonstrates how the understanding and proper manipulation of dimensionality can lead to better data interpretation, improve predictive models, and allow for the visualization of hidden information in high-dimensional datasets. As the field of artificial intelligence progresses, the development and effective implementation of dimensionality reduction techniques will continue to be an area of great interest and importance.

## Chapter 9

Introduction to XAI

Artificial Intelligence (AI) has made tremendous strides in recent years, overcoming challenges that once seemed insurmountable. However, as these systems become increasingly complex and autonomous, a fundamental concern arises: How can we understand the decisions they make? This is at the heart of the Introduction to Explainable Artificial Intelligence (XAI).

As AI systems are integrated into various critical areas such as healthcare, criminal justice, and finance, the transparency and comprehensibility of these systems become essential. The outcomes generated by these models are not always intuitive for humans and are often perceived as "black boxes." It is not enough for a model to provide an answer; it is imperative to understand why it made that decision. In this chapter, we will explore the need for explainability, as well as common techniques in XAI to tackle this challenge.

Need for Explainability

There are several critical reasons why explainability in AI is essential:

Trust and Acceptance

In the realm of AI, trust is paramount. If users and stakeholders cannot understand how an AI came to a conclusion or decision, they are likely to distrust its results. This lack of trust can lead to resistance in adopting new technologies, especially in sensitive domains like healthcare, where decisions can have significant repercussions on people's lives.

Accountability and Ethics

Accountability in automated decision-making is another critical aspect. When an AI model makes an error, such as incorrectly classifying a person as a high crime risk or a patient as healthy, it is crucial to be able to trace the logic behind the decision. A lack of explainability can lead to discrimination, biases, and unfair practices, making developers and organizations accountable for the adverse consequences of their systems.

Regulations and Standards

In some regions, regulations are being implemented that require levels of transparency and explainability in AI systems. For example, the European Union has proposed regulations that mandate that automated decisions can be explained to citizens. This creates an imminent need to design and implement AI models that are not only effective but also understandable.

Continuous Model Improvement

Explainability also plays a vital role in the AI model development lifecycle. By understanding how and why a model makes certain predictions, developers can improve its design and performance. Without this feedback, AI systems may evolve in undesirable directions or fail to adapt to changes in the underlying data.

Common Techniques in XAI

With the importance of XAI well established, let's examine some common techniques and approaches that can help unravel the "black box" of AI models.

Interpretable Models

The most direct way to achieve explainability is to use models that are inherently interpretable. Some examples include:

- **Linear Regressions**: This simple model allows for a quick understanding of the influence of independent variables on the dependent variable. Each coefficient indicates the expected impact on the output given a variation in the input.

- **Decision Trees**: These models split the data based on specific features. The tree structure provides an intuitive visual representation of how decisions are made.

A simple decision tree might look like this:

```
1  [Age]
```

```
2                      /     \
3              <=30        >30
4              /               \
5          [Income]        [Test]
6          /     \         /     \
7      <50K   >=50K   Yes      No
8      /         \       /       \
9    No        Yes   Accept    Reject
```

Decomposition Methods

Decomposition methods are techniques that use more complex models, such as neural networks, and break down their functioning to give meaning to the decisions:

- **SHAP (SHapley Additive exPlanations)**: Utilizes game theory to calculate the contribution of each feature to a model's prediction. This technique allows understanding not only the final decision but also the influence of each variable, providing precise interpretation.

- **LIME (Local Interpretable Model-agnostic Explanations)**: This technique builds a locally interpretable model around the predictions of a complex model. It provides a "local" view of how features influenced a particular decision rather than a global summary.

Decision Visualizations

A powerful way to make AI systems more understandable is through visualizations:

- **Heat Maps**: In the context of neural networks, heat maps can show which parts of the input (for example, regions of an image) have influenced the prediction the most. This can be particularly useful in computer vision problems.

- **Debugging Diagrams**: They provide a graphical way to describe how different features and their interactions contribute to the model's output, allowing users to explore the decisions in detail.

Robustness Testing

The robustness of a model also offers a way to understand its behavior. By testing a model on adversarial or noisy datasets and observing its performance, developers can better comprehend which features are essential for the model's decisions. This helps showcase not only the model's functionality but also its reliability limits.

Common Platform Evaluations

Some platforms are actively working to unify the understanding and application of AI explainability. Tools like **IBM Watson** and **Google Cloud AI** provide frameworks that allow for the implementation of XAI techniques in production models, facilitating organizational adoption.

Conclusions

Explainable Artificial Intelligence is a crucial component for the adoption and trust in AI systems. With the growing concerns about transparency, ethics, and accountability in automated decision-making, it is imperative for developers and organizations to understand and utilize XAI techniques. By doing so, not only do they enhance the trust and comprehensibility of their systems, but they can also contribute to the responsible advancement of AI.

In the world of artificial intelligence, the ability to understand how machines arrive at certain decisions is not just a luxury but a necessity. As we progress through this digital age, the capability to explain and unravel the intricate patterns of AI will be fundamental in building a safer and more reliable future.

## Chapter 10

Case Studies in Explainable AI

Artificial Intelligence (AI) has begun to make significant inroads in various industries, providing solutions that transform the way organizations operate. However, alongside these innovations arises the need to understand the decisions made by AI models. As AI applications become increasingly complex and are deployed in critical contexts, it is essential to examine specific case studies that illustrate the need for and impact of Explainable AI (XAI). In this chapter, we will explore several practical examples of how XAI has been implemented across different sectors, the challenges faced, and the lessons learned.

Case Study 1: Medical Diagnosis with AI

Context

In the healthcare sector, AI systems are being used more and more to aid in clinical decision-making. A prominent example is the use of neural networks to diagnose diseases from medical images, such as X-rays or MRIs. However, the highly critical nature of these decisions demands a level of explainability that can justify the model's recommendations.

Implementation

A hospital utilized an AI system to detect pneumonia from chest X-rays. The AI model was trained with thousands of images, but an XAI module using LIME (Local Interpretable Model-agnostic Explanations) was added. This allowed physicians to obtain explanations about how decisions were made, highlighting specific regions of the images that led to the pneumonia detection.

Results

Physicians not only received predictions but also clear reasons for those decisions, which allowed them to validate and trust the system more. By being able to see the problematic areas of the lungs identified by the model, doctors were able to diagnose and treat patients more effectively, improving clinical outcomes.

Lessons Learned

This case emphasizes the importance of transparency in AI applications in healthcare. The explanations provided by LIME increased physicians' trust in the system, and a positive correlation was observed between trust in the tool and diagnostic accuracy. However, challenges were also identified, such as the need for ongoing supervision and training for doctors to adequately interpret the explanations.

Case Study 2: Credit and Finance

Context

The financial sector faces constant challenges related to credit risk assessment. AI models can predict the likelihood of a credit applicant defaulting on payment, but the implications of these decisions can be significant for both individuals and institutions. Therefore, explainability in credit scoring models is vital.

Implementation

A major banking institution implemented a machine learning model in its risk assessment system. To ensure explainability, the SHAP (SHapley Additive exPlanations) technique was used. This allowed analysts to see exactly how each feature of the applicant influenced the model's decision.

Results

Through the explanations provided by SHAP, analysts were able to identify which factors, such as credit history, income, and debt-to-income ratio, were leading to negative decisions. This visibility not only helped analysts justify decisions to applicants, but also allowed the evaluation processes to be fairer and more equitable, reducing biases that might have influenced the model's decisions.

Lessons Learned

The use of SHAP in the financial sector not only improved the understanding of credit decisions but also helped the institution comply with government regulations that require transparency in decision-making. However, the sector still faces challenges, such as the need to constantly update models to reflect changes in market behavior and the economy.

Case Study 3: Human Resources Sectors

Context

AI has also found its way into talent management, where it is used to analyze resumes and predict job performance. However, the use of AI in this area raises concerns due to its potential to perpetuate existing biases in hiring.

Implementation

A human resources company utilized a classification model to predict which candidates would be most suitable for certain positions. To allow for explainability, they implemented a module that provided interpretations of the model's predictions and highlighted the features that led to the decisions.

Results

The explainability module allowed recruiters to understand why the model recommended certain candidates, helping to identify potential biases in the process. For example, it was noted that the model placed more importance on certain prestigious schools, which did not necessarily correlate with performance.

Lessons Learned

This case demonstrated the need to address biases in AI models in hiring. By providing clear explanations about the model's decisions, recruiters were able to question and adjust the predictions, favoring a more inclusive and fair selection process. Nevertheless, the company recognized that promoting diversity in hiring would require additional efforts beyond the explainability of the model.

Case Study 4: Personalized Marketing

Context

Marketing companies use AI models to personalize campaigns and make recommendations. The ability of a model to explain its decisions is crucial to avoid alienating consumers who feel that the recommendations are irrelevant or invasive.

Implementation

An e-commerce company implemented an AI-based recommendation system. To increase customer trust, they integrated visualization techniques such as heat maps to identify products that were relevant to consumers and explain why certain recommendations were made.

Results

By providing visual explanations of how recommendations were determined, the company observed an increase in conversion rates and a decrease in return rates. Consumers felt more comfortable with the recommendations, as they could see that they were based on their past behaviors and market trends.

Lessons Learned

The use of visual explanations in marketing not only improved the user experience but also led to increased customer satisfaction. However, concerns were raised about data privacy and the need to ensure that information collection was conducted ethically.

Conclusions

These case studies underscore the critical importance of explainability in artificial intelligence applications. By offering clear and understandable explanations, organizations can not only increase trust in their models but also enhance the effectiveness of their impacts in the real world. As AI continues to evolve and occupy a more central role in our lives, the implementation of XAI techniques will be essential to ensure that these technologies are used ethically and responsibly.

Understanding explainable AI is thus not only a technical requirement but also a moral imperative that will clearly benefit various sectors in their journey toward greater transparency and fairness in the use of these powerful tools.

## Chapter 11

Transfer Learning

Transfer learning has emerged as one of the most relevant techniques in the field of artificial intelligence, especially in machine learning and deep learning. This methodology is based on the idea that a model trained on a specific task can be used as a foundation to improve the performance of another model on a different but related task. In this chapter, we will delve into the fundamental concepts of transfer learning, its applications, challenges, and how to implement it effectively in Python.

Fundamental Concepts

Transfer learning is founded on the premise that many machine learning tasks share common characteristics and patterns. By leveraging the knowledge acquired in a previous task, we can reduce the time and resources required to train a new model. This is especially useful when there is limited data available for the new task, but a previously trained model exists on a larger dataset.

Benefits of Transfer Learning

- **Training Efficiency**: Using a pre-trained model can allow the new model to achieve competitive performance with less data and shorter training time.

- **Reduced Risk of Overfitting**: By utilizing a model that has already been trained on a large and diverse dataset, the likelihood of the new model overfitting to a small dataset is minimized.

- **Improved Generalization**: Knowledge transfer can facilitate better generalization to unseen data, especially in related domains.

How Does Transfer Learning Work?

Transfer learning typically follows these steps:

1. **Select a Pre-trained Model**: A model that has been trained on a similar task is chosen. For example, computer vision models like VGG16 or ResNet have been trained on large datasets such as ImageNet.

2. **Adjust the Model**: Depending on the specific task, the pre-trained model may be adjusted for the new task. This may involve adapting the architecture, replacing or adding layers, or simply freezing the initial layers and retraining the upper layers.

3. **Training**: The adjusted model is trained using the new dataset. While some layers may remain frozen (without updating the weights during training), the retrained layers will adapt their weights to better reflect the patterns in the new data.

Applications of Transfer Learning

Transfer learning is applied in various areas, including:

Computer Vision

In computer vision applications, transfer learning has enabled significant advances. By using pre-trained models on tasks such as image classification, object detection, and image segmentation, it is possible to achieve high-precision results on industry-specific datasets with fewer computational resources.

Natural Language Processing

Transfer learning has also gained traction in natural language processing (NLP). Models like BERT and GPT have been trained on large text corpora and then fine-tuned for tasks like sentiment analysis, machine translation, or question answering.

Voice Recognition

In voice recognition, pre-trained neural networks can be adapted to recognize specific accents or dialects, allowing AI systems to be more inclusive and accurate.

Health and Medicine

In the healthcare sector, transfer learning has been used to improve diagnostic models designed to identify diseases from medical images, helping to reduce the time and cost of developing models from scratch.

Implementation Example: Transfer Learning in Python

Next, we will show how to implement transfer learning using a pre-trained model in the context of image classification with TensorFlow and Keras. We will use the ResNet50 model, which has been pre-trained on the ImageNet dataset.

Importing Libraries

First, let's ensure that we have the necessary libraries installed:

```
1  pip install tensorflow numpy matplotlib
```

Transfer Learning Code

Here is the code for an example of transfer learning:

```
1  import numpy as np
2  import matplotlib.pyplot as plt
3  import tensorflow as tf
4  from tensorflow.keras import layers, models
5  from tensorflow.keras.applications import ResNet50
6  from tensorflow.keras.preprocessing.image import
     ImageDataGenerator
7
8
```

```python
    # Load the dataset (assuming we have training and
    validation data)

 9  train_dir = 'path/to/dataset/training'
10  val_dir = 'path/to/dataset/validation'
11
12  # Data preprocessing
13  train_datagen = ImageDataGenerator(preprocessing_function=
    tf.keras.applications.resnet50.preprocess_input)
14  val_datagen = ImageDataGenerator(preprocessing_function=tf.
    keras.applications.resnet50.preprocess_input)
15
16  train_generator = train_datagen.flow_from_directory(
17      train_dir,
18      target_size=(224, 224),
19      batch_size=32,
20      class_mode='categorical')
21
22  val_generator = val_datagen.flow_from_directory(
23      val_dir,
24      target_size=(224, 224),
25      batch_size=32,
26      class_mode='categorical')
27
28  # Load the pre-trained ResNet50 model
29  base_model = ResNet50(weights='imagenet', include_top=False
    , input_shape=(224, 224, 3))
30
31  # Freeze the layers of the base model
32  for layer in base_model.layers:
33      layer.trainable = False
34
35  # Create a new model by adding custom layers
36  x = layers.Flatten()(base_model.output)
37  x = layers.Dense(256, activation='relu')(x)
```

```
38  x = layers.Dropout(0.5)(x)
39  output = layers.Dense(train_generator.num_classes,
     activation='softmax')(x)
40
41  # Build the final model
42  model = models.Model(inputs=base_model.input, outputs=
     output)
43
44  # Compile the model
45  model.compile(optimizer='adam', loss=
     'categorical_crossentropy', metrics=['accuracy'])
46
47  # Train the model
48  history = model.fit(train_generator, validation_data=
     val_generator, epochs=10)
49
50  # Visualize performance
51  plt.plot(history.history['accuracy'], label=
     'training accuracy')
52  plt.plot(history.history['val_accuracy'], label=
     'validation accuracy')
53  plt.title('Model Accuracy During Training')
54  plt.xlabel('Epoch')
55  plt.ylabel('Accuracy')
56  plt.legend()
57  plt.show()
```

Description of the Code

1. **Image Preprocessing**: Using `ImageDataGenerator`, we preprocess the images to ensure they fit the format required by ResNet50.

2. **Load the Pre-trained Model**: We utilize `ResNet50` without the

top part of the model (the classification layers) to use as a base.

3. **Freezing the Base Model**: To ensure that the pre-trained model's layers do not update during training, their weights are frozen.

4. **Adding Custom Layers**: After adding additional layers (such as a dense layer and dropout layer) to adapt the model to the new task, we create the final model.

5. **Training and Evaluation**: The model is trained for a specified number of epochs, allowing the weights of the new layers to be adjusted according to the data.

6. **Performance Visualization**: Finally, we plot the results of accuracy during training and validation, providing a clear insight into the model's performance.

Challenges of Transfer Learning

Although transfer learning presents numerous benefits, it also faces several challenges:

- **Domain Mismatch**: If the domains of the initial and final tasks are very different, the transfer of knowledge may be less effective. For example, training a model on nature images and applying it to medical images may not yield good results.

- **Capacity Overloading**: Freezing too many layers of a pre-trained model might limit the new model's ability to learn task-specific features. A proper balance between frozen and trainable layers is crucial.

- **Hyperparameters**: Selecting hyperparameters for added layers can be challenging. Finding the right number of units in dense layers or dropout rates may require experimentation.

Final Considerations

Transfer learning represents a significant advancement in the development of artificial intelligence models, enabling complex and specific tasks to be performed with less data and training time. As we continue to explore and refine this methodology, it is expected to become a standard tool in the toolbox of AI engineers.

As we have seen throughout this chapter, transfer learning can not only optimize our models but also open new possibilities in the research and application of AI across various industries. As new models are developed and our understanding of how to effectively transfer knowledge improves, we move closer to a future where AI can be used more widely and effectively.

## Chapter 12

Meta-Learning

Meta-learning, often referred to as "learning to learn," is an innovative approach that seeks to improve how artificial intelligence models learn and generalize to new tasks. Instead of focusing solely on optimizing performance on a specific task, meta-learning aims to acquire knowledge on how to learn, which can result in models that quickly adapt to new situations. This chapter will explore the fundamentals of meta-learning, its applications, methods, and practical considerations for effectively implementing it.

Fundamental Concepts

The term "meta-learning" may seem abstract, but it is based on quite intuitive ideas. Unlike traditional learning, where a model is trained to perform a specific task (e.g., image classification), meta-learning focuses on how a model can learn to learn. This involves utilizing experience gained from multiple tasks to improve performance on new tasks.

Analogical Example

Imagine you have a friend who has learned to play several musical instruments, such as the guitar, piano, and drums. If they decide to learn to play the cello, they don't start from scratch. Instead, they can transfer their knowledge of music, such as music theory and motor coordination, to this new skill. Similarly, a meta-learning model applies prior knowledge to adapt its learning to a new dataset or task with a limited number of examples.

Benefits of Meta-Learning

- **Rapid adaptation**: Models can adapt to new tasks with few examples, reducing the need for large amounts of labeled data.

- **Improved generalization**: By learning from multiple tasks, models can identify common patterns and better generalize to unseen situations.

- **Training efficiency**: Reduced training time by minimizing the need for extensive optimization for each particular task.

Types of Meta-Learning

Meta-learning can be classified into three main approaches:

Representation Learning

In this approach, the model learns useful representations of the data that can be applied to multiple tasks. For example, a neural network model that extracts features from images may learn to identify shapes and textures that are essential for both dog and cat classification.

Optimization Learning

This approach focuses on learning how to optimize the parameters of a model. For instance, the optimization algorithm can automatically adjust based on previous tasks, allowing the model to converge more quickly when presented with a new task.

Architecture Learning

Here, models learn what the most suitable architecture is for solving specific tasks. Through experience, a model can discover which types of networks or layers are most effective for certain types of data, thereby optimizing its structure.

Meta-Learning Methods

Below are some of the most popular methods in meta-learning:

MAML (Model-Agnostic Meta-Learning)

MAML is an approach that seeks to train a model to adapt quickly to new tasks with only a few parameter updates. It is based on training an initial model on a variety of tasks, so it can generalize efficiently. The idea is that when presented with a new task, the model can achieve good performance after just a few fine-tuning steps, using a small number of examples.

Example of MAML Implementation in Python

We will use the `torchmeta` library, which facilitates the implementation of meta-learning:

```python
1   import torch
2   import torch.nn as nn
3   from torchmeta.datasets import miniimagenet
4   from torchmeta.utils.data import BatchMetaDataLoader
5
6   # Define a simple model
7   class SimpleCNN(nn.Module):
8       def __init__(self):
9           super(SimpleCNN, self).__init__()
10          self.conv1 = nn.Conv2d(3, 32, kernel_size=3, stride
    =1, padding=1)
11          self.conv2 = nn.Conv2d(32, 64, kernel_size=3,
    stride=1, padding=1)
12          self.fc = nn.Linear(64 * 28 * 28, 10)
    # assumption of input size
13
14      def forward(self, x):
15          x = nn.ReLU()(self.conv1(x))
16          x = nn.ReLU()(self.conv2(x))
17          x = x.view(x.size(0), -1)  # flatten
18          x = self.fc(x)
19          return x
20
21  # Load a sample dataset for miniimagenet
22  dataset = miniimagenet.MiniImagenet(subset='train',
    transform=None)
23
24  # Define a meta-dataloader
25  meta_loader = BatchMetaDataLoader(dataset, batch_size=16)
26
27  # Initialize the model
28  model = SimpleCNN()
29  optimizer = torch.optim.Adam(model.parameters(), lr=0.001)
30
31  # Training process (simplified)
```

```
32  for batch in meta_loader:
33      # Here goes the training process using MAML
34      pass
```

Prototypical Networks

Prototypical networks are another common approach based on the idea of creating a prototype or "central representation" for each class in a latent space. For a new task, the model calculates the distance between a new example and these prototypes to classify the example into the nearest class.

Essentially, prototypical networks transform examples into a space where classes are represented by their centroids, improving the model's ability to generalize to unseen classes.

Few-Shot Learning Techniques

Few-shot learning is a closely related area to meta-learning. Few-shot learning methods seek to train models that can make accurate predictions from a very limited number of examples. This is particularly useful in situations where acquiring large amounts of labeled data is costly or impractical.

For example, a few-shot learning model could be used to identify rare plant species from a few available images, utilizing its prior knowledge about other similar species.

Applications of Meta-Learning

Meta-learning has many applications across various fields:

Computer Vision

In computer vision, meta-learning models can adapt to new object classes from only a few images. This is useful in robotics applications, where a robot may need to recognize and manipulate previously unseen objects in its environment.

Natural Language Processing

In the field of natural language processing, meta-learning models allow systems to understand and adapt to new languages or text analysis tasks with just a limited number of examples, enhancing their versatility.

Medical Diagnosis

Meta-learning holds the promise of accelerating learning in the medical field, where models can learn to diagnose conditions from only a few cases, optimizing their ability to generalize to different types of patients.

Challenges of Meta-Learning

Despite its benefits, meta-learning also presents several challenges:

- **Task Mismatch**: If the initial tasks are not aligned with the new task, the model may not generalize adequately.

- **Computational Complexity**: Training meta-learning models can be computationally intensive, as they often require training on multiple tasks simultaneously.

- **Hyperparameter Selection**: Finding the right set of hyperparameters for learning and adaptation can be complicated.

Conclusions

Meta-learning represents an exciting and promising approach in the field of artificial intelligence. By focusing on learning the most efficient way to learn, this approach has the potential to transform how AI models are developed and used across various applications. As research advances and techniques are refined, meta-learning could be the key to building more robust and adaptive artificial intelligence systems that can effectively operate in dynamic and ever-changing environments.

## Chapter 13

Introduction to Language Models

In the last decade, language models have transformed the way we interact with technology and have revolutionized the field of natural language processing (NLP). From automatic translation systems to virtual assistants, these models are fundamental for understanding and generating human language text. In this chapter, we will explore the fundamentals of language models, their evolution, the different types of models, and their practical applications.

What is a Language Model?

A language model is a system that assigns probabilities to sequences of words in a language. Simply put, its goal is to predict the likelihood that a word or a sequence of words will appear in a certain context. This is used for various tasks in text processing, such as completing sentences, translating text, generating content, and performing sentiment analysis.

Analogous Example

Imagine you have a friend who is a great joke teller. Every time you say "What do you call a dog that does magic?", he already anticipates that you should expect "a labracadabrador." In this case, your friend acts as a language model: he has prior knowledge about the words and structures commonly used in jokes to anticipate the correct answer.

Evolution of Language Models

n-gram Models

The earliest language models were based on the n-gram technique, which considers the probabilities of a word given its immediate context in the form of sequences of n words. In practice, this means that a 2-gram or bigram model focuses on pairs of words, while a 3-gram model considers triples of words.

The basic infrastructure for an n-gram model is as follows:

1. **Corpus Construction**: A large set of text is chosen to analyze the frequencies of the n-grams.

2. **Probability Calculation**: The relative frequencies of each n-gram's occurrence in the corpus are calculated.

3. **Predictions**: To predict the next word, the existing n-grams are searched, and the one with the highest probability is selected.

Limitations: n-gram models suffer from issues such as data sparsity (they cannot generalize well to unseen contexts) and are unable to capture long-term dependencies in the text.

Neural Network-Based Models

With the advancement of neural networks, language modeling techniques have evolved. Neural network-based language models are capable of learning richer and deeper representations of language.

1. **Word Embeddings**: Before attention mechanisms or transformers existed, more advanced techniques like Word2Vec and GloVe were introduced, which convert words into high-dimensional vectors, capturing semantic relationships. For example, the distance between "king" and "queen" is similar to the distance between "man" and "woman."

2. **Recurrent Neural Networks (RNNs)**: RNNs were integrated as a way to model language by manipulating sequences. RNNs can maintain the context of previous words through a feedback loop that allows the model to remember previous information.

3. **Long Short-Term Memory (LSTM)**: A variant of RNNs specifically designed to address the vanishing gradient problem in long sequences. LSTMs can learn and remember long-term dependencies, thus improving the model's predictive capability.

Transformers

The revolution in language models began with the introduction of transformers in the paper "Attention is All You Need." This approach marked a significant difference in how sequences are handled in NLP.

1. **Attention**: Instead of relying on the sequential structure of RNNs, transformers use attention mechanisms that assign weights to different parts of the input, allowing the model to focus on the most relevant words for prediction.

2. **Parallel Training**: Unlike RNNs, which require sequential

processing, transformers can process all words in the sequence simultaneously, speeding up training time.

3. **BERT Model**: Bidirectional Encoder Representations from Transformers is an innovative model whose bidirectional approach allows it to understand the full context of a word in a sentence rather than being limited to previous or subsequent words. BERT has become a standard in various NLP applications.

4. **GPT (Generative Pre-trained Transformer)**: Unlike BERT, which focuses on understanding language, GPT specializes in generating natural language. Through unsupervised learning on large amounts of text, GPT can generate coherent and relevant text.

Applications of Language Models

Language models have applications in numerous fields. Some of the most notable include:

Automatic Translation

The ability to understand and generate language makes language models essential for automatic translation. Tools like Google Translate use advanced models that can translate between multiple languages while maintaining the fluency of the text.

Virtual Assistants

Virtual assistants like Siri, Alexa, and Google Assistant rely on language models to understand voice commands, answer questions, and perform tasks. The smooth interaction between the user and the assistant is based on natural language understanding.

Sentiment Analysis

Companies use language models to analyze customer comments and opinions on social media and product reviews. Sentiment modeling allows organizations to receive real-time feedback on their products and services.

Content Generation

Language models like GPT-3 can generate coherent content in various formats, from articles to stories. This has opened up new possibilities in writing and automated content creation.

Automatic Summarization

The process of summarizing long documents can be efficiently performed by trained language models. This is useful in business and academic environments where extracting key information from large volumes of text is required.

Conclusions

Language models have developed astonishing capabilities and are a fundamental part of the revolution we are experiencing in artificial intelligence. As technology advances, we are likely to see even more advanced models that expand our abilities in understanding and generating human language.

The future of language models is promising, with applications in various fields and a significant impact on how we communicate and work. As we continue to explore and refine these models, it is also essential to address ethical considerations, such as inherent biases in training data and the implications of automatic content generation. Responsibility and transparency are critical as we advance in this exciting and challenging machine learning discipline.

## Chapter 14

GPT (Generative Pre-trained Transformer)

In the field of natural language processing (NLP), one of the most significant advancements has been the emergence of transformer-based models, especially the GPT (Generative Pre-trained Transformer) model. GPT has revolutionized text generation and taken language automation to unprecedented levels. In this chapter, we will explore the architecture, functionality, and practical applications of GPT, along with its evolution and the challenges it faces today.

GPT Architecture

GPT is an autoregressive language model that uses transformer architecture. The main innovation of the transformer architecture is its attention mechanism, which allows models to weigh different parts of the input more effectively. This contrasts with traditional models based on recurrent neural networks (RNN), which process text sequentially and are susceptible to the vanishing gradient problem.

The basic structure of GPT consists of the following key elements:

Attention Mechanism

The attention mechanism is fundamental to the transformer. Instead of processing words sequentially, attention allows the model to consider all the words in the input simultaneously, assigning different weights to each based on its relevance.

For example, in the sentence "The dog barked because it saw a cat," the word "because" establishes a causal relationship between "barked" and "saw." The attention mechanism will enable the model to focus its attention on "barked" while evaluating "because," thus improving its understanding of the context.

Embedding Layer

GPT begins text processing by converting words into high-dimensional vectors, known as embeddings. This vector representation captures semantic and syntactic relationships between words. For instance, the words "king" and "queen" will have vector representations that are close to each other, allowing the model to comprehend that both words are related.

Transformer Layers

The core of GPT consists of multiple stacked transformer layers. Each layer contains two main subcomponents:

1. **Multi-Head Attention Layer**: Allows the model to capture relationships between multiple parts of the text across different attention subspaces. This is crucial for understanding the

complexities of natural language.

2. **Feed-Forward Layer**: Applied to the results of the attention layer, it transforms this data through nonlinear functions, thereby enhancing the model's ability to learn complex representations.

The outputs from these layers are normalized and passed to the next stage, enabling the model to gain a deeper understanding of the language structure.

Decoding Process

GPT is an autoregressive model that generates one word at a time. The text generation process starts with a prompt or initial input, and the model predicts the next word based on the previous context. This approach is iteratively repeated to generate complete text sequences.

Training GPT

The training of GPT occurs in two stages: pre-training and fine-tuning.

Pre-training

During this phase, GPT is fed large quantities of unlabeled text from diverse sources, such as books, articles, and websites. The goal of the model is to learn the probabilities of words in a given context, optimizing its ability to predict the next word in the sequence. The loss function commonly used is cross-entropy.

Fine-Tuning

After pre-training, GPT is fine-tuned for specific tasks. This involves training the model on a labeled dataset for a particular task, such as sentiment analysis, machine translation, or text generation on a specific topic. This phase helps the model specialize and improve its performance on specific tasks.

Applications of GPT

The versatility of GPT makes it suitable for a wide range of applications in the field of NLP:

Text Generation

GPT is widely used for generating coherent and contextually relevant text. It can be utilized in applications that require content creation, such as articles, reports, or narratives. For example, GPT might be prompted to continue a story started by an author, achieving a fluid and creative continuation.

Virtual Assistants

Intelligent virtual assistants can leverage GPT to generate responses to questions naturally. This enhances the user experience, as interactions become more satisfying and natural. GPT's capability to understand the intent behind questions allows for more accurate and helpful responses.

Machine Translation

Although GPT was not specifically designed for translation, its ability to handle complex contexts makes it useful for this task. It can generate quality translations by capturing the nuances of language and providing translations that sound natural.

Sentiment Analysis

GPT can be trained to detect sentiments in a text, classifying it as positive, negative, or neutral. This is invaluable for companies seeking to measure public perception of their brand or product.

Automatic Summarization

GPT can summarize long articles or extensive documents into more concise and manageable versions. This is particularly useful in situations where information needs to be digested quickly, such as in business or academic settings.

Challenges and Ethical Considerations

Despite its power and versatility, GPT and other language models face significant challenges:

Data Bias

As GPT is trained on large volumes of text extracted from the web, it may incorporate biases present in that data. This can result in generating biased or inappropriate content. Working towards mitigating these biases is crucial for developing responsible applications that do not perpetuate misinformation or prejudices.

Misinformation

GPT's ability to generate convincing text also raises concerns about its use for generating misleading content or propaganda. As models like GPT are implemented, it is vital to establish regulations and ethical practices to prevent misuse.

Scalability and Resources

Models like GPT require significant computational resources, which can limit accessibility and feasibility for smaller organizations or startups. Seeking ways to optimize models or utilize lighter versions is an active area of research.

Conclusions

GPT represents a monumental advancement in the field of natural language processing and has transformed the way we interact with machines. From its ability to generate coherent and relevant text to its application in various NLP tasks, GPT has proven to be an impressive tool.

As we continue to explore and improve these models, it is essential to address the ethical and technical considerations that arise, ensuring that their development and use are carried out responsibly. With the ongoing evolution of AI, the potential of GPT and other similar models is astounding, providing unparalleled opportunities in the creation, communication, and understanding of human language.

## Chapter 15

BERT (Bidirectional Encoder Representations from Transformers)

The BERT model (Bidirectional Encoder Representations from Transformers) has marked a milestone in the field of natural language processing (NLP). Developed by Google and presented in 2018, BERT has transformed the way models understand the context of language, enabling significant advances in various NLP tasks, from text classification to question answering. In this chapter, we will explore the architecture and functioning of BERT, as well as its applications and advantages over previous approaches, such as unidirectional models.

What is BERT

BERT is a language model based on the transformer architecture, designed to understand text in a bidirectional context. Unlike earlier models that read text in a single direction (left to right or right to left), BERT considers the information from all words in a sentence simultaneously. This allows it to capture complex relationships and the full meaning of a word based on the surrounding words.

Analogous Example

Imagine you are reading the sentence "The bank was full of people." Without the full context, it might be confusing to determine whether "bank" refers to a financial institution or a place where people sit. However, by analyzing the sentence as a whole, one can deduce that it refers to a physical place. BERT, being a bidirectional model, is capable of understanding these nuances of meaning that depend on context.

BERT Architecture

BERT is built on the transformer architecture and uses a combination of attention and feed-forward layers to process text. Here we break down the key components of BERT:

Transformer Layers

BERT employs multiple stacked transformer layers, each composed of two subcomponents:

- **Multi-Head Attention Layer**: This layer allows the model to pay attention to different parts of the input simultaneously. By distributing attention over several "heads," the model can capture different aspects of the relationships between words. For example, it might focus on the relationship between "bank" and "people" in one head, while another head deals with "full" and "of".

- **Feed-Forward Layer**: After the attention layer, the data is transformed through a fully connected neural network, allowing the model to learn non-linear representations of the relationships between words.

Word Inputs and Masks

BERT takes inputs in the form of sentence pairs, enabling the model to learn not only from a single sentence but also from its relationship to another. Words are converted into embedding vectors that represent their contextual meanings. Additionally, BERT uses a technique called "masking" where some words in the input text are hidden during training, forcing the model to predict the masked words based on the remaining context. This is known as "mask language modeling" (MLM).

Tokenization

The input to BERT is processed through a tokenization step, where the text is converted into tokens (units of meaning) that can be individual words or parts of words (sub-words). BERT utilizes WordPiece tokenization, which allows it to handle rare or unknown words by breaking them down into more common subunits.

BERT Training Process

The training of BERT occurs in two main stages:

Pre-training

During this phase, the model is trained on large volumes of unlabeled text, such as Wikipedia and books, using two tasks:

- **Masked Language Model (MLM)**: As mentioned earlier, some words in the input are masked, and the model must predict them from the context. This helps the model learn robust representations of words based on their context.

- **Next Sentence Prediction (NSP)**: This task involves predicting whether one sentence follows another in the text. This helps BERT understand the relationship between sentences, which is crucial for tasks like sentence pair classification.

Fine-tuning

After pre-training, BERT is fine-tuned for specific tasks. During this phase, the model is trained on a labeled dataset for the task at hand, be it text classification, question answering, or sentiment analysis. The model adapts and optimizes to improve its performance on that particular task.

Applications of BERT

Since its introduction, BERT has proven effective in a variety of natural language processing applications:

Text Classification

BERT can be used to classify documents, emails, or comments into specific categories. For instance, a fine-tuned model on product review data can classify a comment as positive, negative, or neutral.

Question Answering

In question-answering tasks, BERT can understand the question and search for relevant answers in a given context. For example, when asked "What is the capital of France?", BERT uses its contextual intelligence to find the correct answer in a text corpus.

Sentiment Analysis

BERT-based models are effective at detecting the sentiment behind a text. By analyzing comments on social media or reviews, BERT can classify sentiments as positive, negative, or neutral, helping companies gauge the public perception of their products.

Machine Translation and Text Generation

BERT has been utilized as part of machine translation and text generation systems, where its contextual understanding improves the quality of translations and content generated by the model.

Advantages of BERT over Previous Models

BERT introduces several improvements over previous models, such as unidirectional models and n-gram based approaches:

- **Deep Contextual Understanding**: By analyzing context in a bidirectional manner, BERT captures the meaning of words better based on their context, which is key to understanding complex languages.

- **Flexibility Across Tasks**: BERT is a versatile model that can be fine-tuned for different NLP tasks with minimal modifications to the architecture, reducing the need to design task-specific models.

- **Improved Performance**: In various competitions and standard evaluations, BERT has outperformed previous models, setting new records in NLP benchmark tasks.

Challenges and Limitations of BERT

Despite its advantages, BERT also presents challenges:

Resource Requirements

Training BERT models from scratch can require powerful hardware and large amounts of data, which can be a limitation for smaller organizations.

Data Bias

Like other language models, BERT can inherit and amplify biases present in the training data. This underscores the importance of using representative datasets and diverse techniques to mitigate biases.

Interpretability

The increased complexity of these models also poses challenges in terms of interpretability. Understanding how and why a model arrives at certain predictions can be difficult, which can be critical in applications where transparency is essential.

Conclusions

BERT has revolutionized the field of natural language processing by changing the way models understand and generate text. Its capacity to grasp context at a deeper level has enabled improvements in numerous NLP applications. As we continue to explore new architectures and optimizations, BERT remains a key benchmark in the research and development of AI technologies focused on language, helping us create more natural and effective interactions between humans and machines.

## Chapter 16

Robotics and Artificial Intelligence

The intersection of robotics and artificial intelligence (AI) represents one of the most exciting and promising areas of modern technology. Robotics, understood as the construction and use of robots to perform specific tasks, combined with AI, which gives machines the ability to interact, learn, and make decisions, has led to significant advancements in various industries. In this chapter, we will explore how AI is applied in robotics, its applications, the challenges faced, and the future trends that are shaping this fascinating discipline.

The Convergence of Robotics and AI

Traditional robotics has largely been conceived as a discipline centered on mechanics and control. However, with the incorporation of artificial intelligence, robots are now capable of performing complex tasks that require not only physical action but also information processing, decision-making, and learning from environmental data. This shift has enabled robots to adapt and respond more effectively to dynamic and unstructured situations.

How AI Enhances Robotics

AI enhances robotics in several key ways:

Perception

Perception refers to a robot's ability to interpret data from the surrounding world. Using machine learning techniques and computer vision, robots can analyze images and sensory data in real-time. For example, a robot working in a warehouse environment can use cameras and sensors to identify and classify different types of objects, allowing it to make more informed decisions about what to pick and where to place items.

Perception Example

Suppose we are designing a robot for fruit classification in a warehouse. By using computer vision algorithms, the robot can identify different fruits based on their color, shape, and size. By processing images of the fruits through a trained model, the robot can quickly determine whether a fruit is an apple or an orange, increasing its efficiency compared to manual methods.

```
1   import cv2
2   from tensorflow.keras.models import load_model
3
4   # Load a pre-trained model for fruit classification
```

```
5   model = load_model('fruit_classifier_model.h5')
6
7   # Function to make predictions on images
8   def predict_fruit(image_path):
9       image = cv2.imread(image_path)
10      image = cv2.resize(image, (100, 100))
11      image = image.astype('float32') / 255.0
    # Normalization
12      image = image.reshape(1, 100, 100, 3)
    # Reshape for the model
13      prediction = model.predict(image)
14      class_name = ['Apple', 'Orange', 'Banana'][prediction.
    argmax()]
15      return class_name
16
17  # Usage example
18  result = predict_fruit('path/to/fruit.jpg')
19  print(f"The fruit is: {result}")
```

Decision Making

Decision making is another crucial aspect where AI has had an influence. By using reinforcement learning algorithms, robots can learn to optimize their behavior through experience. For example, a robot navigating an unknown environment can use this approach to learn the best path to avoid obstacles and reach its goal.

Decision Making Example

Imagine a mobile robot designed to explore a maze. By using reinforcement learning algorithms, the robot can automatically learn the best way to navigate the paths of the maze through interaction with its environment, receiving rewards when it reaches its goal and penalties when it bumps into a wall.

```python
1  import random
2
3  class MazeRobot:
4      def __init__(self):
5          self.position = (0, 0)  # Initial position
6          self.history = []  # Movement history
7
8      def move(self, direction):
9          # Simple simulation of movement in a maze
10         if direction == 'up':
11             self.position = (self.position[0], self.
   position[1] - 1)
12         elif direction == 'down':
13             self.position = (self.position[0], self.
   position[1] + 1)
14         elif direction == 'left':
15             self.position = (self.position[0] - 1, self.
   position[1])
16         elif direction == 'right':
17             self.position = (self.position[0] + 1, self.
   position[1])
18         self.history.append(self.position)
19
20         return self.position
21
22     def explore(self):
23         for _ in range(10):  # 10 random moves
24             direction = random.choice(['up', 'down', 'left'
   , 'right'])
25             print(f"Moving: {direction}, New position: {
   self.move(direction)}")
26
```

```
27  # Usage example
28  robot = MazeRobot()
29  robot.explore()
```

Learning and Adaptation

The ability of robots to learn from past experiences and adapt to new scenarios is one of the most striking elements of AI in robotics. Through the use of machine learning algorithms, robots can improve their performance over time. For example, a cleaning robot can optimize its cleaning route as it learns about the layout of furniture and the dirtiest areas.

Applications of AI-Driven Robotics

The combination of robotics and artificial intelligence has a wide range of applications across various industries:

Manufacturing

In manufacturing, AI-driven robots can perform tasks such as assembly, quality control, and inventory management. Thanks to their learning capabilities, they can adapt to changing tasks and different products without the need for intensive reprogramming. This translates into increased productivity and reduced costs.

Healthcare

Healthcare robotics is experiencing significant growth. AI-assisted surgical robots can perform procedures with high precision, improving patient outcomes. Additionally, assistive robots can help elderly or disabled individuals with their daily tasks, providing a higher level of autonomy.

Agriculture

Agricultural robotics employs drones and autonomous vehicles with AI capabilities to plant, monitor, and harvest crops. These robots can identify pests, manage irrigation, and optimize pesticide use, contributing to more efficient and sustainable farming.

Logistics

In logistics, robotics and AI are used for warehouse automation and inventory management. Robots can move autonomously within the warehouse space, manage storage, and perform deliveries, optimizing time and reducing operational costs.

Space Exploration

Robotics also plays a crucial role in space exploration, with rovers and probes designed to collect data and samples on planets and moons. These robots use AI to make real-time decisions, explore new environments, and send data back to Earth.

Challenges in AI-Driven Robotics

Despite impressive advancements, several challenges and obstacles must be addressed in the context of AI-driven robotics:

Safety

Safety is a critical concern in robotics, especially in environments where robots interact with humans. Ensuring that robots operate safely and without causing harm is a complex task that requires careful design and extensive testing.

Ethics

Ethical considerations related to the use of robots are also fundamental. As we adopt robots into everyday life, it's essential to think about how these devices should be used and how biases in their decisions can be prevented.

Complexity of Decision Making

Real-world situations are often complex and dynamic. Training robots to make effective decisions in changing and non-predefined conditions remains a hot topic of intense study and development.

Human-Robot Interaction

The ability for robots to effectively interact with humans and respond to their behaviors and emotions is a challenging research area. Developing intuitive interfaces and improving natural language understanding is key to the acceptance of robotics in society.

Future of Robotics and AI

The future of robotics and artificial intelligence is promising. The combination of these two disciplines is expected to continue transforming industries, improving efficiency and quality of life. Some emerging trends include:

- **Collaborative Robots (Cobots)**: Designed to work alongside humans, these robots use AI to interact safely and efficiently, sharing spaces and tasks.

- **Explainable AI**: The need for robots to make transparent and understandable decisions is becoming increasingly important to gain public trust.

- **Development of Smart Materials**: As soft robotics advances, new materials are being researched that allow robots to physically adapt to their environment.

- **Autonomous Robotics**: The evolution toward increasingly autonomous robots will be key in areas such as delivery and transportation, where minimizing human involvement is sought.

Conclusions

The interaction between robotics and artificial intelligence is reshaping the future of multiple sectors, providing innovative and efficient solutions to complex problems. With the continuous evolution of technology, it is crucial to address both the challenges and opportunities that arise. As we move toward a more automated future, the collaboration between humans and machines will become an essential element of everyday life, enhancing our ability to tackle global challenges and improving the quality of life worldwide.

## Chapter 17

Internet of Things (IoT)

The Internet of Things (IoT) has become one of the most revolutionary trends in the field of technology. The ability to interconnect devices and sensors through the Internet has allowed for the creation of smarter and more efficient environments. In this chapter, we will explore the concept of IoT, how it works, its applications, challenges, and how artificial intelligence (AI) integrates into this ecosystem.

What is the Internet of Things?

The Internet of Things refers to the network of physical objects that are equipped with sensors and software that enable them to connect and exchange data with other devices and systems through the Internet. These objects can be anything from household appliances and vehicles to industrial sensors and medical devices. IoT transforms everyday objects into smart devices that can collect, send, and receive data.

Analogous Example

Imagine a house where the appliances are connected to the Internet. If your refrigerator can communicate information about the stored food and its freshness status, it can send you a notification when items are about to expire. This not only optimizes food management but also reminds you that you need to buy certain products. This is a simple example of how IoT can combine with technology to facilitate daily life.

How Does IoT Work?

The functioning of IoT is based on several key components:

Sensors and Devices

IoT devices are equipped with sensors that collect data from the environment. These sensors can measure temperature, humidity, motion, light, pressure, and much more. This data is sent through communication networks to be processed and analyzed.

Connectivity

Connectivity is crucial in IoT. Devices can connect to the Internet in various ways, whether via Wi-Fi, Bluetooth, Zigbee, Sigfox, or cellular networks. This connectivity allows devices to exchange data in real-time.

Data Processing

The data collected by IoT devices is often sent to the cloud for processing.

In the cloud, algorithms and machine learning models are used to analyze and extract useful information from that data. This information can then be used to make automated decisions or for manual analysis by users.

User Interface

Finally, the results of data processing are presented to users through graphical interfaces. These interfaces can be mobile applications, online dashboards, or notification systems that alert users about relevant events.

Applications of IoT

IoT has applications across a wide variety of sectors:

Smart Homes

Smart homes are one of the most visible examples of IoT. Devices such as smart thermostats, connected lights, and security cameras can be controlled remotely. For example, an automated irrigation system can adjust the amount of water supplied based on soil moisture, thus optimizing water usage.

Health

In the healthcare sector, IoT has led to the implementation of connected medical devices, such as vital sign monitors that send real-time data to healthcare providers. This allows for more detailed patient monitoring and quicker response in critical situations.

Industry 4.0

Industry has adopted IoT to create smart factories. Monitoring devices and connected equipment allow companies to optimize their production processes and reduce downtime. For instance, a machine that monitors its own performance can send alerts before a failure occurs, enabling operators to act preventively.

Smart Agriculture

Agriculture also benefits from IoT through the use of sensors that monitor soil conditions, weather conditions, and crop growth. This enables farmers to make informed decisions about irrigation, fertilization, and harvesting, thus increasing yield and sustainability.

Smart Cities

IoT is applied in urban planning through the development of smart cities where traffic systems, public lighting, and waste management are interconnected. For example, traffic lights can adjust their change time based on traffic density, improving traffic flow and reducing CO_2 emissions.

AI Integration in IoT

The combination of IoT and AI has the potential to take automation and intelligence to new levels. AI can analyze large volumes of data generated by IoT devices, providing valuable insights and real-time decision-making capabilities.

Practical Application Example

For example, consider a healthcare system that uses wearable devices to monitor patients' activity and vital signs. These devices can send data to the cloud, where an AI model can analyze the information for patterns indicating health issues. If anomalies are detected, the system can automatically alert medical personnel to initiate intervention.

Example Code in Python

Using a library like `scikit-learn`, a simple classification model can be implemented to predict a patient's health based on data such as heart rate, blood pressure, and activity levels. Here is an example:

```python
import pandas as pd
from sklearn.model_selection import train_test_split
from sklearn.ensemble import RandomForestClassifier
from sklearn.metrics import accuracy_score

# Let's assume we have a dataset with patient information
data = pd.read_csv('patient_data.csv')

# Define the target variable and independent variables
X = data[['heart_rate', 'blood_pressure', 'activity_level']]
y = data['health']  # 0 = healthy, 1 = illness

# Split the data into training and testing sets
X_train, X_test, y_train, y_test = train_test_split(X, y, test_size=0.3, random_state=42)

# Create and train the model
model = RandomForestClassifier(n_estimators=100)
model.fit(X_train, y_train)
```

```
19
20  # Make predictions and evaluate the model
21  y_pred = model.predict(X_test)
22  accuracy = accuracy_score(y_test, y_pred)
23
24  print(f'Health model accuracy: {accuracy:.2f}')
```

Challenges of IoT

Despite its benefits, IoT also faces several challenges:

Security and Privacy

The interconnection of devices poses significant risks, including cyberattacks and privacy violations. The security of transmitted and stored data is paramount. For example, a poorly secured IoT device can be hacked and used to access sensitive information.

Interoperability

The diversity of IoT devices and communication protocols makes interoperability a challenge. Ensuring that different devices from different manufacturers can work together is essential to maximize the effectiveness of IoT.

Data Management

The massive amount of data generated by IoT devices can be overwhelming. Analyzing, storing, and efficiently managing this data is an important challenge that needs to be addressed.

Scalability

As the number of IoT devices grows, so does the demand for infrastructure and processing capacity. Planning the scalability of these networks is fundamental for the future of IoT.

Conclusions

The Internet of Things is transforming the way we interact with the world around us, providing new opportunities for efficiency and intelligence across various sectors. The integration of AI in IoT promises to take this revolution even further, enabling more informed decisions and advanced automation. However, it is crucial to address the associated challenges, such as security and interoperability, to fully leverage the advantages of IoT. By doing so, we can build a more connected and efficient future where devices and systems work together to improve our quality of life.

## Chapter 18

Introduction to Anomaly Detection

Anomaly detection is a crucial component in the field of artificial intelligence and machine learning, with applications ranging from cybersecurity to health monitoring and fraud detection. In this context, an anomaly refers to a pattern in a dataset that deviates significantly from what is expected. This chapter aims to provide an introduction to anomaly detection, its types, methods, applications, and challenges.

What is Anomaly Detection?

Anomaly detection, also known as outlier detection, involves identifying data points that do not fit an expected pattern. These outliers can indicate issues such as errors in data collection, fraud, or system failures. By recognizing these anomalies, organizations can make more informed and proactive decisions to address underlying problems.

Analogous Example

Imagine you are monitoring an athlete's performance in a race. Suppose that in most competitions, the athlete finishes the race in an average time of 10 minutes. However, on one occasion, they finish in 15 minutes. This finishing time could be considered an anomaly. A possible injury, a technical issue, or unusual race conditions might have occurred. Recognizing this type of anomaly can help determine the cause and prevent similar problems in the future.

Types of Anomalies

There are several classifications of anomalies, which can help determine the appropriate approach for their detection. Below are the most common categories:

Outliers

Outliers are individual observations that deviate significantly from the rest of the data. For example, if we record the monthly income of a group of employees and one of them reports an income of 1 million dollars, this value is likely an outlier.

Contextual Anomalies

Contextual anomalies are cases where a point may be standard in one context but is considered anomalous in another. For instance, a temperature of 30 degrees may be normal in summer but anomalous in winter.

Collective Anomalies

Collective anomalies are patterns of abnormal behavior in a group of observations. For example, a group of users showing an unusual change in their purchasing patterns may be considered anomalous collectively, even though the individuals are not outliers separately.

Methods for Anomaly Detection

There are several approaches and techniques for detecting anomalies, which can be classified into statistical methods, machine learning-based methods, and data mining-based methods.

Statistical Methods

Statistical methods rely on assumptions about the distribution of data. For example:

- **Standard Deviation**: A threshold can be established based on the mean and standard deviation. If a point is more than 3 standard deviations from the mean, it may be considered an anomaly.

```python
import numpy as np

# Example data
data = np.array([1, 2, 2, 3, 4, 5, 100])  # 100 is an outlier

# Calculate mean and standard deviation
mean = np.mean(data)
std_deviation = np.std(data)

```

```
10  # Identify anomalies
11  upper_threshold = mean + 3 * std_deviation
12  anomalies = data[data > upper_threshold]
13
14  print(f"Identified outliers: {anomalies}")
```

Machine Learning-Based Methods

Machine learning methods are used to detect anomalies without assuming a specific distribution of the data. Some popular techniques include:

- **Decision Trees**: These can be used to classify points as normal or anomalous based on the characteristics of the data.

- **Support Vector Machines (SVM)**: SVM can be tuned to detect anomalies by identifying a separating margin between the classes.

```
1   from sklearn.svm import OneClassSVM
2
3   # Training data (normal points)
4   X_train = np.array([[0], [0.1], [0.2], [0.3], [0.4], [0.5],
    [1], [1.1], [1.2]])
5
6   # Train the model
7   model = OneClassSVM(gamma='auto').fit(X_train)
8
9   # New data for prediction
10  new_data = np.array([[0], [0.1], [0.3], [1.5]])
    # 1.5 is an anomaly
11  predictions = model.predict(new_data)
12
13  # Results
14  print(f"Predictions: {predictions}")
```

```
# -1 indicates anomaly, 1 indicates normal
```

Data Mining-Based Methods

These methods involve using clustering techniques and unsupervised analysis. For example:

- **K-Means**: Through clustering, the distance between points can be analyzed to recognize those far from their centroids.

- **Principal Component Analysis (PCA)**: Reduces the dimensionality of the data and allows the identification of anomalies by observing projections in a lower-dimensional space.

Applications of Anomaly Detection

Anomaly detection has applications in numerous fields:

Cybersecurity

In cybersecurity, anomaly detection helps identify unusual activities that may indicate a hacking attempt or a data breach. Monitoring systems can alert administrators when they detect unusual traffic patterns.

Finance

Fraud detection in financial transactions is used to identify unauthorized charges or suspicious behavior. Anomaly detection tools can flag transactions that are out of the ordinary for review.

Health

In the healthcare domain, monitoring systems can identify anomalous patterns in patients' vital signs, which may indicate medical issues requiring immediate intervention.

Predictive Maintenance

In industry, anomaly detection is used for predictive maintenance of machinery, identifying patterns that could precede technical failures, allowing interventions before problems occur.

Quality Control

Quality control systems in factories can detect anomalies in production that could result in defective products, allowing for real-time adjustments.

Challenges in Anomaly Detection

Despite its utility, anomaly detection presents several challenges:

Dataset Complexity

Datasets can be complicated and contain noise or variability that may hinder the identification of anomalies. Careful preprocessing and feature selection are required.

Threshold Design

Establishing appropriate thresholds to differentiate between normal and anomalous data can be challenging, both in statistical methods and machine learning.

Interpretation

Understanding why a point is considered anomalous and the underlying cause can be complicated. Tools that provide explanations for the decisions made by models should be considered.

Conclusions

Anomaly detection is a fascinating field that offers powerful tools for identifying hidden problems across a variety of contexts. As artificial intelligence and machine learning evolve, the techniques and tools for anomaly detection also advance, providing organizations with the capability to proactively respond to unusual events. By addressing the inherent challenges in this field, it is possible to enhance reliability, efficiency, and safety across multiple industries.

## Chapter 19

Techniques and Algorithms for Anomaly Detection

Anomaly detection is a growing area within machine learning and encompasses a variety of techniques and algorithms that permit the identification of unusual patterns in data. These patterns can signal critical issues, fraud, system failures, or significant changes in the behavior of a system. In this chapter, we will analyze some of the most common techniques and algorithms used in anomaly detection, how they work, and practical implementation examples.

Statistical Methods

Statistical methods are one of the most basic and traditional approaches for anomaly detection. They rely on assumptions about the distribution of the data and allow for the establishment of thresholds that define whether a point is normal or anomalous.

Standard Deviation

A common way of detecting anomalies is using standard deviation. A dataset typically behaves within a range of standard deviations from the mean. If a point falls beyond a specified threshold (for example, 3 standard deviations), it is considered anomalous.

Example in Python:

```python
import numpy as np

# Sample data
data = np.array([10, 12, 12, 13, 12, 11, 14, 100])  # 100 is an outlier

# Calculation of mean and standard deviation
mean = np.mean(data)
std_deviation = np.std(data)

# Identifying anomalies
upper_threshold = mean + 3 * std_deviation
anomalies = data[data > upper_threshold]

print(f"Identified outliers: {anomalies}")
```

In this example, the data is analyzed to determine if there are outlying values that are more than three standard deviations from the mean.

Box Plot

Another statistical technique used to detect anomalies is the box plot. The box plot visualizes the distribution of data and allows for the identification of outliers based on quartiles.

$IQR = Q3 - Q1$ A point is considered an outlier if it is above $Q3 + 1.5 \times IQR$ or below $Q1 - 1.5 \times IQR$.

Implementation Example:

```python
1  import matplotlib.pyplot as plt
2
3  # Sample data
4  data = [1, 2, 2, 3, 4, 5, 100]
5
6  # Create a box plot
7  plt.boxplot(data)
8  plt.title('Box Plot of Data')
9  plt.show()
```

The box plot visually displays the distribution and allows for intuitive identification of anomalies.

Machine Learning-Based Methods

While statistical methods are useful, they are often surpassed by the complexity of data in real-world scenarios. For this reason, machine learning algorithms are frequently applied for anomaly detection.

Support Vector Machines (SVM)

Support Vector Machines (SVM) are used for classifying data and can be adapted for anomaly detection. In particular, One-Class SVM is trained using only normal data to identify anomalies as those points that lie far from the boundary created by the normal data.

Example of using One-Class SVM in Python:

```
1   from sklearn.svm import OneClassSVM
2   import numpy as np
3
4   # Training data (normal points)
5   X_train = np.array([[0], [0.1], [0.2], [0.3], [0.4], [0.5],
    [1], [1.1], [1.2]])
6
7   # Model training
8   model = OneClassSVM(gamma='auto').fit(X_train)
9
10  # New data for prediction
11  new_data = np.array([[0], [0.1], [0.3], [1.5]])
    # 1.5 is an anomaly
12  predictions = model.predict(new_data)
13
14  # Results
15  print(f"Predictions: {predictions}")
    # -1 indicates anomaly, 1 indicates normal
```

In this case, the SVM uses "normal" points to define what constitutes acceptable behavior and then identifies any new point that is outside of that definition.

Clustering Algorithms

Clustering algorithms are useful for detecting anomalies by identifying points that do not fit into any of the formed clusters. K-Means is a commonly used algorithm that can help identify outlying points based on the distance to the cluster centroids.

Example in Python:

```
1   from sklearn.cluster import KMeans
```

```
2
3   # Sample data
4   data = np.array([[1], [2], [2], [3], [4], [5], [100]])
    # 100 is an anomaly
5
6   # Apply K-Means
7   kmeans = KMeans(n_clusters=2)
8   kmeans.fit(data)
9   points = np.array(data).flatten()
10  labels = kmeans.labels_
11
12  # Identifying anomalies (using distance to the centroid)
13  centroids = kmeans.cluster_centers_
14  distance_to_centroids = np.linalg.norm(data - centroids[
    labels], axis=1)
15
16  # Distance threshold to identify anomalies
17  distance_threshold = 10  # Arbitrarily selected
18  anomalies = data[distance_to_centroids > distance_threshold
    ]
19
20  print(f"Identified outliers: {anomalies.flatten()}")
```

This approach uses K-Means to assign labels to the data and then calculates the distance of each point to its corresponding centroid to determine if it exceeds a predefined threshold.

Neural Network-Based Methods

As technology has advanced, methods based on neural networks for anomaly detection have also been developed. A popular approach is using Autoencoders.

Autoencoders

Autoencoders are neural networks used to learn an efficient representation of the data. They consist of two main parts: the encoder, which maps the input data to a lower-dimensional space, and the decoder, which attempts to reconstruct the original data.

Autoencoders are particularly useful for anomaly detection because, when trained on normal data, they can easily reconstruct those inputs. However, when faced with anomalous data, the network may struggle more to reconstruct them, resulting in a higher reconstruction error.

Example in Python:

```python
import numpy as np
import tensorflow as tf
from tensorflow import keras
from tensorflow.keras import layers

# Normal training data
X_train = np.array([[0], [0.1], [0.2], [0.3], [0.4], [0.5]]
)

# Define the Autoencoder model
autoencoder = keras.Sequential([
    layers.Dense(2, activation='relu', input_shape=(1,)),
    layers.Dense(1, activation='sigmoid')
])

autoencoder.compile(optimizer='adam', loss='mse')

# Train the Autoencoder
autoencoder.fit(X_train, X_train, epochs=100, verbose=0)

```

```
20  # New data (including an anomaly)
21  new_data = np.array([[0], [0.1], [0.3], [1.5]])
    # 1.5 is anomalous
22  reconstructions = autoencoder.predict(new_data)
23
24  # Calculate reconstruction error
25  errors = np.mean(np.square(new_data - reconstructions),
    axis=1)
26
27  # Threshold to define anomalies
28  error_threshold = 0.1  # Arbitrarily chosen
29  anomalies = new_data[errors > error_threshold]
30
31  print(f"Identified outliers: {anomalies.flatten()}")
```

This code implements a simple autoencoder that, when trained on a set of normal data, allows for detecting points that deviate from this normal behavior.

Applications of Anomaly Detection

The techniques and algorithms mentioned have applications across various industries:

- **Cybersecurity**: Detecting unauthorized access and fraud.

- **Finance**: Identifying fraudulent transactions and suspicious activities.

- **Healthcare**: Monitoring unusual vital signs that could indicate medical issues.

- **Manufacturing**: Quality monitoring in production, identifying defective products.

- **IoT**: Monitoring connected devices to detect anomalous

behaviors.

Challenges in Anomaly Detection

Methods for anomaly detection face multiple challenges:

- **Computational Cost**: Some algorithms, especially those based on deep learning, can be resource-intensive.

- **Threshold Selection**: Establishing appropriate thresholds can be complicated; thresholds that are too low may result in false alarms, while thresholds that are too high may overlook significant anomalies.

- **Interpretability**: Understanding why a point was classified as anomalous can be difficult, particularly with complex algorithms like neural networks, complicating their use in critical applications where transparency is essential.

Conclusions

Anomaly detection plays a fundamental role in identifying issues across multiple fields. As we move forward, techniques and algorithms continue to evolve, and the integration of new machine learning approaches is expanding the possibilities for effective detection. It is crucial for organizations to understand the tools available and how to apply them effectively to ensure ongoing operation and integrity of their processes.

## Chapter 20

Applications of AI in the Business World

Artificial intelligence (AI) is profoundly transforming the business environment, offering new opportunities to improve efficiency, optimize processes, and foster innovation. As companies seek to adapt to an increasingly competitive and dynamic market, the integration of AI-based technologies has become a key factor for success. This chapter will explore various applications of AI in the business world, focusing on process automation and business process improvement.

Process Automation

Process automation refers to the use of technology to perform tasks that were previously carried out by humans. AI, along with other technologies such as robotics and management software, enables organizations to automate repetitive and rule-based processes, resulting in greater efficiency and cost reduction.

Examples of Process Automation

Customer Service

Customer service is one of the sectors that benefits the most from AI-driven automation. The implementation of chatbots and virtual assistants allows companies to provide 24/7 support without the need for constant human intervention. These systems can answer frequently asked questions, direct users to relevant resources, and handle simple inquiries.

Example of a Chatbot in Python

Below is a simple code for a chatbot using the `ChatterBot` library, which allows for creating conversation-oriented chatbots:

```
1  from chatterbot import ChatBot
2  from chatterbot.trainers import ChatterBotCorpusTrainer
3
4  # Create a new chatbot
5  chatbot = ChatBot('MyBot')
6
7  # Train with Spanish data
8  trainer = ChatterBotCorpusTrainer(chatbot)
9  trainer.train('chatterbot.corpus.spanish')
10
11 # Conversation with the chatbot
12 while True:
13     user_input = input("You: ")
14     response = chatbot.get_response(user_input)
15     print(f"MyBot: {response}")
```

This code sets up a basic chatbot that can interact and learn from conversations by being trained with a Spanish corpus. This type of technology enables companies to handle high volumes of inquiries without the need for additional human resources.

Document Processing

Automation of document processing is another area where AI can make a significant difference. Technologies like optical character recognition (OCR) and natural language processing (NLP) can be used to extract information from scanned or unstructured documents, which can then be processed and stored in structured databases.

Example of OCR in Python

Here is an example of using `pytesseract`, a Python library for performing OCR on images:

```
1  import pytesseract
2  from PIL import Image
3
4  # Load the image
5  image = Image.open('document.png')
6
7  # Perform OCR
8  extracted_text = pytesseract.image_to_string(image, lang=
     'spa')
9
10 print(f"Extracted text: \n{extracted_text}")
```

This code takes an image of a document and uses OCR to extract the text, which can then be further processed and analyzed by the organization.

Advantages of Process Automation

- **Efficiency and Productivity**: By automating repetitive tasks, employees can focus on more strategic activities, thus increasing overall productivity.

- **Reduced Errors**: Automation reduces the likelihood of human errors in routine tasks, improving the quality of work.

- **Decreased Costs**: Reducing human workload can lead to decreased operational costs, which is especially valuable for small and medium enterprises.

- **Improved Customer Experience**: Faster and more efficient customer service increases customer satisfaction, which can lead to greater loyalty and customer acquisition.

Business Process Improvement

In addition to automation, AI can enhance existing business processes by analyzing large volumes of data, identifying patterns, and offering recommendations based on that data.

Predictive Analysis

Predictive analysis consists of using AI techniques and machine learning to predict future outcomes based on historical data. This is especially useful in areas such as sales, marketing, and inventory management.

Example of Predictive Analysis with Linear Regression in Python

Using the `scikit-learn` library, a linear regression model can be implemented to forecast future sales:

```python
1   import numpy as np
2   import pandas as pd
3   from sklearn.model_selection import train_test_split
4   from sklearn.linear_model import LinearRegression
5   import matplotlib.pyplot as plt
6
7   # Create a sample dataset
8   data = {
9       'marketing_expenses': [100, 150, 200, 250, 300],
10      'sales': [10, 20, 25, 30, 50]
11  }
12  df = pd.DataFrame(data)
13
14  # Split data into training and testing sets
15  X = df[['marketing_expenses']]
16  y = df['sales']
17  X_train, X_test, y_train, y_test = train_test_split(X, y,
    test_size=0.2, random_state=42)
18
19  # Create and train the model
20  model = LinearRegression()
21  model.fit(X_train, y_train)
22
23  # Predict
24  predictions = model.predict(X_test)
25
26  # Plot results
27  plt.scatter(X, y, color='blue', label='Actual data')
28  plt.plot(X_test, predictions, color='red', label=
    'Prediction')
29  plt.xlabel('Marketing Expenses')
30  plt.ylabel('Sales')
31  plt.legend()
32  plt.show()
```

This code trains a model to predict sales based on marketing expenses and visualizes the results. Such a model allows companies to make more informed decisions regarding resource allocation.

Personalization of Customer Experience

AI enables companies to deliver personalized experiences to their customers by analyzing their behavior and preferences to provide tailored recommendations.

Example of a Recommendation System

Recommendation systems are widely used on platforms like Amazon and Netflix. Here is a simple example of a recommendation system using collaborative filtering:

```python
from sklearn.metrics.pairwise import cosine_similarity
import numpy as np

# Sample user and product data
user_products = np.array([[5, 3, 0, 1],
                          [4, 0, 0, 1],
                          [1, 1, 0, 5],
                          [0, 0, 5, 4]])

# Calculate similarities using cosine similarity
similarities = cosine_similarity(user_products)

# Display similarity matrix
print("Similarity matrix:\n", similarities)
```

This code calculates the similarity between different users' preferences to recommend products based on others' experiences with similar tastes.

Advantages of Business Process Improvement

- **Data-Driven Decisions**: Companies can make more informed and strategic decisions thanks to real-time data analysis.

- **Increased Sales**: By personalizing the customer experience, companies can boost conversion rates and customer satisfaction.

- **Continuous Improvement**: With predictive analysis, companies can adapt more quickly to changing market trends, ensuring they remain competitive.

Conclusions

Artificial intelligence is revolutionizing the business world, offering tools and technologies that enable process automation, improve efficiency, and provide more personalized experiences to customers. From automated customer service to predictive analysis, AI applications have the potential to transform how companies operate and compete in the market. As technology continues to evolve, it is crucial for organizations to stay abreast of these innovations and seek opportunities to integrate AI into their operations, ensuring their growth and long-term sustainability.

## Chapter 21

Predictive Maintenance

Predictive maintenance has become a key strategy in modern industry, allowing organizations to maximize operational efficiency and reduce costs. This methodology is based on the collection and analysis of data to anticipate failures in equipment and machinery before they occur, which facilitates proactive planning and scheduling of maintenance. Throughout this chapter, we will explore the fundamentals of predictive maintenance, its importance, the technologies involved, practical applications, and the challenges it faces.

What is Predictive Maintenance?

Predictive maintenance is a strategy that uses real-time data and data analysis to predict when a failure is likely to occur in an asset or equipment. Unlike reactive maintenance, which is based on wear and failure of systems, or preventive maintenance, which is carried out at regular intervals without considering the condition of the equipment, predictive maintenance focuses on the current health of assets. This allows for informed decision-making about the optimal time to perform maintenance, minimizing downtime and reducing unnecessary costs.

Example Analogy

Imagine you own a car. Instead of taking it to the mechanic every six months (preventive maintenance) or waiting for it to break down (reactive maintenance), you decide to install a monitor that constantly assesses the health of the engine and can predict when certain components are reaching the end of their useful life. With this information, you can schedule an appointment with the mechanic just before a failure occurs, ensuring that your car keeps running smoothly.

Importance of Predictive Maintenance

Implementing predictive maintenance strategies offers multiple key benefits for organizations:

- **Cost Reduction**: By anticipating failures and scheduling maintenance at optimal times, companies can avoid costs associated with emergency repairs and unplanned downtime.

- **Increased Operational Efficiency**: A proactive approach allows maintenance to be integrated more efficiently into workflows, improving the availability and utilization of equipment.

- **Improved Equipment Lifespan**: Predictive maintenance encourages timely interventions in equipment, which in turn extends their lifespan and enhances overall performance.

- **Safety**: The reduction in equipment failure rates not only optimizes production but also improves employee safety by preventing accidents related to machinery failures.

Technologies Involved in Predictive Maintenance

Predictive maintenance relies on several key technologies that enable data collection and analysis:

IoT (Internet of Things)

IoT sensors are installed on equipment and machinery to monitor constants such as temperature, vibration, pressure, and other operational parameters. These sensors collect real-time data, which is then transmitted to analysis platforms over the Internet.

Data Analysis and Machine Learning

Data analysis techniques are crucial for extracting useful information from the large volumes of data collected by sensors. Machine learning algorithms can be trained to identify patterns correlating certain indicators with impending failures.

Predictive Models

Predictive models, using statistical or machine learning algorithms, allow for forecasting the failure time of equipment based on historical data and behavior.

Predictive Analysis Example with Machinery

Suppose we are monitoring an electric motor. Below is an example in Python of how we could use a simple linear regression model to predict the lifespan of a motor based on historical data:

```python
import numpy as np
import pandas as pd
from sklearn.model_selection import train_test_split
from sklearn.linear_model import LinearRegression
import matplotlib.pyplot as plt

# Create a sample dataset
# Data representing hours of usage and failures occurred
data = {'hours_usage': [100, 200, 300, 400, 500, 600, 700,
800, 900, 1000],
        'failures': [1, 2, 1, 3, 5, 6, 5, 7, 9, 10]}
df = pd.DataFrame(data)

# Split the data into training and testing sets
X = df[['hours_usage']]
y = df['failures']
X_train, X_test, y_train, y_test = train_test_split(X, y,
test_size=0.2, random_state=42)

# Create and train the linear regression model
model = LinearRegression()
model.fit(X_train, y_train)

# Make predictions
predictions = model.predict(X_test)

# Visualize the results
plt.scatter(X, y, color='blue', label='Actual Data')
```

```
27  plt.plot(X_test, predictions, color='red', label=
    'Predictions')
28  plt.xlabel('Hours of Usage')
29  plt.ylabel('Failures')
30  plt.legend()
31  plt.title('Prediction of Failures Based on Hours of Usage')
32  plt.show()
```

This code allows us to visualize how the number of failures in an electric motor can depend directly on usage hours. This can help to schedule maintenance just before expected issues arise, optimizing action.

Applications of Predictive Maintenance

The applications of predictive maintenance are diverse and present in many sectors:

Manufacturing

In manufacturing plants, the incorporation of predictive maintenance helps monitor critical machines and tools for production, preventing disruptions in workflow. By predicting failures in equipment such as presses or lathes, factories can ensure that production remains on track and uninterrupted.

Energy

Energy sector companies use predictive maintenance to monitor generators and turbines. The data analysis collected from these machines can alert about abnormal conditions, preventing outages and ensuring continuous power supply.

Aerospace

In the aerospace industry, predictive maintenance is essential for safety. Aircraft are equipped with numerous sensors that evaluate their condition and allow airlines to schedule maintenance before catastrophic failures occur, thus ensuring passenger safety.

Healthcare

In healthcare, medical equipment like MRIs and CT scanners can benefit from predictive maintenance. This ensures that machines are operational and ready for use in critical moments, enhancing patient care.

Challenges of Predictive Maintenance

Despite its benefits, predictive maintenance faces several challenges:

Data Collection

Installing sensors and collecting real-time data can be costly and require adequate infrastructure. Organizations must be willing to make significant initial investments.

Complex Data Analysis

As large volumes of data accumulate, analyzing it becomes more complex and may require specialized skills in data science. This often means that companies need to invest in additional training and resources.

Resistance to Change

The implementation of predictive maintenance practices may face cultural challenges within organizations. Shifting from a traditional approach to a data-driven one can be complicated and generally requires a change in mindset and work practices.

Impact on the Workforce

There may be concerns about how predictive maintenance impacts the workforce. Some employees may fear that automation and AI technologies will reduce job opportunities. However, predictive maintenance can also create new opportunities by allowing more strategic roles in data management and analysis.

Conclusions

Predictive maintenance represents a significant advancement in how organizations manage their assets. By leveraging technology and data, companies can stay ahead of problems, optimizing operations and improving the effectiveness of their processes. As technologies continue to evolve, the adoption of predictive maintenance will become a standard in the industry, ensuring not only the sustainability of assets but also a more efficient and effective management of resources. Through careful implementation and addressing its inherent challenges, organizations can greatly benefit from this innovative strategy.

## Chapter 22

Ethics in AI

Artificial intelligence (AI) is significantly transforming modern society, impacting everything from the way we work to our daily interactions. However, as these technologies advance, important ethical concerns also arise. This chapter will focus on the fundamental ethical principles that should guide the development and use of AI, as well as relevant case studies that illustrate the ethical challenges faced by this discipline.

Fundamental Ethical Principles

Ethics in AI is a growing and dynamic field that encompasses several key principles:

Justice

One of the most important aspects of ethics in AI is justice. AI systems must be developed and deployed in a way that does not perpetuate existing biases or create new forms of discrimination. This includes ensuring that algorithms are fair and do not favor one group over another. For example, in the financial sector, it is crucial that AI models used to assess creditworthiness do not exclude specific populations due to biases in the training data.

Analogical Example:

Imagine a basketball game where the referee tends to favor certain teams. This leads to biased foul calls that affect the outcome of the game. Similarly, if an AI system has biases, it could discriminate in important decisions like loan approvals, causing certain groups to be disproportionately disadvantaged.

Transparency

Transparency refers to the need for AI systems to be understandable and subject to auditing. Developers must be able to explain how and why an algorithm makes particular decisions. A lack of transparency can lead to distrust in the technology, as users may question the justification behind the results.

Example Code:

The library LIME (Local Interpretable Model-agnostic Explanations) in Python allows for creating local explanations of AI model predictions. Below is an example of how it could be used to better understand how a classification model makes decisions:

```
1  import numpy as np
2  import pandas as pd
3  import lime
4  from lime.lime_tabular import LimeTabularExplainer
5  from sklearn.ensemble import RandomForestClassifier
6  from sklearn.model_selection import train_test_split
```

```
7
8  # Sample data
9  data = pd.read_csv('customer_data.csv')
   # Load a fictional dataset
10 X = data.drop('outcome', axis=1)
11 y = data['outcome']
12
13 # Split the data
14 X_train, X_test, y_train, y_test = train_test_split(X, y,
     test_size=0.2, random_state=42)
15
16 # Create model
17 model = RandomForestClassifier()
18 model.fit(X_train, y_train)
19
20 # Create LIME explainer
21 explainer = LimeTabularExplainer(X_train.values,
     feature_names=X_train.columns, class_names=['No', 'Yes'],
     mode='classification')
22
23 # Choose an example to explain
24 explanation = explainer.explain_instance(X_test.values[0],
     model.predict_proba, num_features=5)
25
26 # Show the explanation
27 explanation.show_in_notebook()
```

Responsibility

Responsibility implies that developers and organizations implementing AI must be accountable for the decisions made by their systems. If an AI causes harm, it is essential to determine who is responsible, be it a developer, a company, or an institution. Creating a legal and policy framework that clearly defines who is responsible will facilitate an ethical use of AI.

Analogical Example:

Imagine an autonomous vehicle that has an accident. Determining who is responsible for the actions of the car—the manufacturer, the software developer, or the owner—is key to understanding who should take the blame. Likewise, in AI, guidelines must be established to determine responsibility when an AI system makes a decision that causes harm.

Privacy

AI often requires large amounts of data to learn and improve. This raises concerns about user privacy. The collection and use of personal data must be handled with the utmost caution. Organizations should be transparent about how data is collected, stored, and used, and must implement security measures to protect sensitive information.

Code Example:

To exemplify privacy protection in data handling, here is a basic example of how to anonymize data in a Python DataFrame using `pandas`:

```
1  import pandas as pd
2
3  # Load a fictional dataset
4  data = pd.read_csv('people_data.csv')
5
6  # Anonymize data by removing sensitive information
7  anonymized_data = data.drop(['name', 'address'], axis=1)
8
9  # Save the anonymized dataset
10 anonymized_data.to_csv('people_data_anonymized.csv', index=
       False)
```

Case Studies in AI Ethics

Over the years, several case studies have emerged that illustrate these ethical principles in action, as well as their transgressions.

Facial Recognition Case

Facial recognition has been controversial due to accuracy issues and racial biases. Several studies have shown that facial recognition algorithms often have significantly higher error rates for Black individuals and for women compared to white men. This has raised concerns about discrimination and excessive surveillance.

Judicial Systems Case

In some judicial systems, algorithms have been used to predict the likelihood of recidivism among offenders. These tools have been criticized for perpetuating racial biases, as they may be based on historical data that reflects inequalities in the justice system. As a result, some offenders may face longer sentences or stricter parole conditions based on biased predictions.

Customer Service Chatbots Case

Some chatbots were designed to solve common customer service issues, but users began to notice responses that contained racial and gender biases. This led companies to rethink how these models are trained and to implement stricter policies regarding the language and responses they generate.

Conclusions

Ethics in artificial intelligence is essential for the responsible and sustainable development of this technology. The principles of justice, transparency, responsibility, and privacy must guide every aspect of the AI lifecycle. As we move towards a more AI-driven future, it is crucial for developers, companies, and society as a whole to collaborate in establishing an ethical framework that enables the use of AI in a fair and beneficial manner for all.

Adopting a proactive approach to ethics in AI will not only help to avoid potential issues and crises but also foster public trust in these technologies, leading to broader and more positive adoption of AI-based solutions.

## Chapter 23

Future Challenges of AI

Artificial intelligence (AI) has made impressive advancements in recent years, transforming entire industries and the way we interact with technology. However, as we move into an AI-driven future, we also face significant challenges that must be addressed to ensure these technologies are implemented ethically and effectively. This chapter will explore emerging trends in AI, the challenges we confront, and the final considerations we should keep in mind.

Emerging Trends in AI

The field of artificial intelligence is constantly evolving, and various trends are shaping its future. Some of the most notable include:

Explainable AI (XAI)

As AI models become more complex, the need for these machines to be understandable to humans arises. Explainable AI (XAI) aims to make the decisions made by algorithms more transparent and comprehensible. This is essential in applications where the ability to make ethical decisions is critical, such as in healthcare, criminal justice, and finance.

Analogous Example:

Imagine a doctor using a machine to diagnose diseases. If the machine indicates that a patient has a serious illness, the doctor must understand why the machine arrived at that conclusion to effectively communicate it to the patient and make informed decisions about their treatment.

Federated Learning

Federated learning is a trend that allows AI models to be trained without the need to centralize data on a single server. Instead, algorithms are trained on local devices, meaning that the data never leaves the user's device. This approach protects the privacy and security of sensitive data while enabling models to benefit from a wide range of data.

Python Example:

Below is a brief example of how an application might implement a federated learning scheme using the `PySyft` library, which enables collaborative training of AI models in a private manner:

```
1  import syft as sy
2  import torch
3
4  # Create a network of workers
5  hook = sy.TorchHook(torch)
6  alice = sy.VirtualWorker(hook, id='alice')
7  bob = sy.VirtualWorker(hook, id='bob')
8
9  # Suppose we have a sample dataset
```

```
10  data_alice = torch.tensor([[1.0, 2.0], [1.0, 3.0]],
        requires_grad=True).send(alice)
11  data_bob = torch.tensor([[1.0, 4.0], [1.0, 5.0]],
        requires_grad=True).send(bob)
12
13  # Sample models
14  model = torch.nn.Linear(2, 1)
15
16  # Training function in a federated setting
17  def federated_train(model, data):
18      model.send(data.location)
19      predictions = model(data)
20      return predictions.get()
21
22  # Training on local devices
23  result_alice = federated_train(model, data_alice)
24  result_bob = federated_train(model, data_bob)
25
26  print(f"Alice's Predictions: {result_alice}")
27  print(f"Bob's Predictions: {result_bob}")
```

Artificial General Intelligence (AGI)

The quest for artificial general intelligence (AGI), which refers to the ability of a machine to understand or learn any intellectual task that a human can perform, remains a topic of debate and speculation. Although we are still far from achieving AGI, research in this area will continue, raising important questions about control, ethics, and how we will interact with machines that have human-level intelligence.

Fostering Interdisciplinarity

AI will not be effectively applied without working together with other disciplines like sociology, law, ethics, and psychology. Interdisciplinary collaboration is vital for tackling complex problems and understanding how technology influences human life.

Challenges in AI Implementation

As the use of AI becomes more prevalent, we also face several challenges.

Data Bias

AI models are only as good as the data used to train them. If the data is biased, AI is likely to make biased decisions. To prevent this, it is essential to apply bias mitigation methodologies in data collection and model training.

Bias Example:

Consider an algorithm used to select candidates for a job. If the model was trained on historical data that reflects workplace biases, it could discriminate against candidates from underrepresented groups, perpetuating inequality.

```
1   # Example of bias mitigation through data regulation
2   import pandas as pd
3
4   # Sample data with bias
5   data = pd.DataFrame({
6       'candidate': ['A', 'B', 'C', 'D'],
7       'experience': [5, 3, 8, 2],
8       'gender': ['M', 'F', 'M', 'F'],
```

```
 9        'accepted': [1, 0, 1, 0]
10  })
11
12  # Method to remove gender information from the data
13  data_without_gender = data.drop('gender', axis=1)
14
15  print(data_without_gender)
```

Data Privacy and Security

With the increasing amount of data generated and used by AI systems, concerns arise about how this data is managed. Organizations must adopt robust data protection practices and be transparent about how data is collected and used.

Job Displacement

Automation and the use of AI across various industries pose the risk of job displacement. It is crucial for companies to address this challenge proactively by providing opportunities for re-skilling and adapting their workforce to the new roles that will emerge.

Final Considerations

The future of artificial intelligence is both promising and challenging. As this technology continues to evolve, organizations, developers, and policymakers must work together to address the ethical and technical challenges that arise. Transparency, fairness, and privacy protection must be cornerstones in the development of AI systems.

It is essential that we are prepared to adapt and evolve in this ever-changing environment. Building a future where AI benefits society as a whole will be a collective effort, and the dialogue around AI ethics must be continuous. Interdisciplinary collaboration, education on AI challenges, and commitment to robust ethical standards will be fundamental in our pursuit of a smarter and more equitable future. By confronting these challenges, we can ensure that artificial intelligence is a powerful ally in building a better world.